THE PHYSICAL EDUCATION CURRICULUM IN THE SECONDARY SCHOOL: PLANNING & IMPLEMENTATION

THE PHYSICAL EDUCATION CURRICULUM IN THE SECONDARY SCHOOL: PLANNING & IMPLEMENTATION

Gordon L Underwood
Nonington College
Dover

The Falmer Press
A member of the Taylor & Francis Group

First published 1983

ISBN 0 905273 47 8 (paper)
0 905273 48 6 (cased)

Phototypeset in Linotron 202 by
Graphicraft Typesetters Hong Kong

Jacket illustration by Helen Underwood
Jacket design by Leonard Williams

Printed by Taylor and Francis (Printers) Ltd
Basingstoke, England
for
The Falmer Press
Falmer House
Barcombe
Lewes, Sussex
BN8 5DL

Contents

Contents

Tables

Tables

Appendices

Acknowledgements

This study has taken several years to complete and I am indebted to my colleagues and friends, too many to mention by name, in lecturing, advising and teaching who have sustained and motivated me during this time. I am especially grateful to those teachers who agreed to be interviewed in relation to their planning procedures and to those members of the physical education profession who ensured such a high return for the questionnaire. Without their generous co-operation, none of this would have been possible.

Foreword

It is with a high degree of pleasure that I write this Foreword for I have known Gordon Underwood over many years and am aware of the industry and care that have gone into the compilation of this text. I hope that the Foreword will be read and the text will be studied since it portrays an overall view of the current approach to Physical Education/Movement Studies in this country and all of us who are associated with these subjects should have knowledge of the general presentation that is now being made.

There are many broad statements about teaching, but one that is undoubtedly true is that the proper teaching of any subject is a time consuming occupation. With regard to Physical Education/Movement Studies, this time is spent not only with the regular classes but also with the development of teams and individuals, with after school clubs and with week-end commitments. These conditions involve long hours of effort usually with emphasis on practical work. For a great number of teachers, practical work assumes major importance and, in contrast, the planning of the curriculum with all its ramifications, becomes scrambled in at odd opportunities. This is not to deny the existence of organization and some approach to planning but it seems to take second place in our work and is often done without the same enthusiasm as is applied to the practical situation.

Perhaps the practical emphasis that is so characteristic of our efforts indicates that we like doing things at which we are good, and basically we are excellent practitioners, highly capable of dealing adequately with direct teaching situations and with appropriate content of lessons. If criticism can be levelled at us, it can possibly be directed towards some inadequacies regarding the planning and development of syllabuses, the statements about outcomes and objectives associated with our courses and the accurate assessment of our levels of success. It may be assumed by us that any weaknesses in organized planning can be counterbalanced by enthusiasm displayed towards the practical but this must be considered as a strange anomaly for it means that we are trying to produce excellence without the proper framework of approach in the planning stages. It means also that our understanding of curriculum planning as the real basis of the work we do is neither comprehended nor appreciated and that the environment of activity that we have created is not completely in accord with acceptable educational principles.

In his book, Gordon Underwood has probed this imbalance between practical and planning and regarding planning itself, the main results he says '... have suggested that there was a great diversity and many omissions in the presentation of the syllabuses.' He also says, 'The review of literature suggests that there is no single way in which teachers plan their courses' and 'Teachers would welcome some guidance in their curriculum planning.' These conclusions which have real bearing on our present situation are some of the resultants from several years of research which has included a national survey covering 608 schools representative of all areas of the country together with direct interviews with Heads of sixteen Physical Education/Movement Studies Departments.

The results of both the survey and the interviews have been carefully analyzed and fair conclusions have been drawn regarding planning, development, organization and assessment, all of which are items pertaining to the understanding and application of the ideas of curriculum theory. These facts are reported in the text and from this evidence we can become aware of the way in which we set about our work. The evidence reveals that we place great store on the development of skill, we emphasize the importance of the content of lessons and we are cognisant of the value of leisure, fitness and socialization. To our credit also, we plan the compulsory core of work efficiently and there is adequate checking by Heads of Departments to ensure that the syllabus as planned is being implemented.

However, a query may be interposed at this juncture for there may be many interpretations as to the content and amplitude of a syllabus. It may merely be a general programme of work that has become established by tradition and is applicable in outline to classes of differing abilities, or it may consist of a listing of intentions, broad headings and progressions. If this is the basis of our planning, it is just about adequate as a syllabus but if it is considered to be a curriculum it omits items like objectives and outcomes, varied and appropriate teaching approaches, the right sort of lesson content to achieve the objectives and the important aspect of evaluation. The implication is that well considered planning may rarely be present in our work.

There is also evidence from the results of the survey that when activities are introduced in a more recreative fashion as applies in the higher classes of the school, these optional activities are less subject to planning than was the approach during the core curriculum period. Obviously recreation and leisure activities are of importance but a purely recreational method which is basically activity may be deemed to belittle our standing as teachers of an educational subject.

The text as previously indicated, reviews many aspects of our present situation and it has been mentioned that we should all be associated with this knowledge. No current text outlines our position more thoroughly and as such the book should be recommended reading for all students of Physical Education/Movement Studies and for teachers in our profession.

It should be stated that there may be good reasons for our reluctance to use the curriculum models suggested by educational theorists for we may have considered them to be time consuming and unworkable. This is perhaps a fair criticism, but our answer should not be to reject curriculum ideas outright but to come up with a model which is adaptable to our purpose and is professionally acceptable. At present we may only be on the fringe of this development for it is reported in the text that as part of the enquiry an attempt was made to collect written syllabuses from ninety Secondary Schools. Only twenty syllabuses were returned and the deduced reasons were that they did not exist in written form in the other seventy schools or that they would not bear scrutiny. This is further evidence of the need for planned organization.

As well as allowing us to make a re-appraisal of ourselves, the book places the ball right in our court and indicates steps that should be taken for the development of our subject. The evidence gives us praise and offers criticism, the future as always is up to us.

Joe Jagger
Westgate-on-Sea
August, 1982

1 Curriculum Planning and Physical Education

One of the main aims of this book is to investigate the ways in which teachers plan and implement the physical education curriculum in secondary schools. In addition, it also attempts to examine the relationship between these planning procedures and the theoretical approaches to curriculum planning. The book is based on one of the few physical education curriculum research projects carried out in the last few years and involved talking to teachers as well as examining the planning procedures in the school situation.

During the past two decades, there have been many curriculum projects in this country, mainly sponsored by the Schools Council. A large number of these projects have been directed towards specific subjects (*e.g.* Engineering Science, 1970–1981; Geography for the Young School Leaver, 1970–1981); whereas others have a more general application to the curriculum (*e.g.* Middle Years of Schooling, 1968–1972; Evaluation and the Teacher, 1978–1986). Apart from 'Physical Education in Secondary Schools' (1970–1971), none were specifically directed towards physical education. Nevertheless, this broad approach in curriculum research has made physical education teachers aware of the importance of curriculum planning and has put some pressure on them to be more clear and more effective regarding their overall programmes.

The actual construction of a physical education curriculum is a demanding task which all teachers should accept as part of their professional responsibility. Ideally, the planning must provide a sense of direction and purpose to teaching and learning situations which will enable staff and pupils to be clear about what they are trying to achieve. At present, there is no central reference to guide and assist teachers in this process. In addition, the knowledge concerning the methods teachers use in their preparation is sparse and this was emphasized recently when, regarding subjects generally, Clark and Yinger (1979) stated, 'At this time we know very little about why teachers plan, how teacher planning changes with experience and whether individual differences influence the quantity and style of planning'. There would, therefore, appear to be a dearth of evidence regarding this form of preparation.

All curriculum construction should normally involve the teacher in a consideration of the aims and objectives of the subject, a selection of subject matter and the teaching and learning experiences he wishes to give to the children, together with some form of evaluation. It is not easy to plan and organize such important areas in a logical manner and it may be that some aspects are given greater emphasis than others, or perhaps even omitted altogether. There is evidence by Taylor (1970), in his book entitled *How Teachers Plan Their Courses*, which indicates that teachers adopt a rather unsystematic approach. This is somewhat surprising considering the importance of planning in the curriculum process. Whether or not these comments are applicable to physical education is not known, as the extent to which teachers of physical education plan and implement their curriculum in secondary schools has not been the subject of a major study.

The first task in any study of this nature must be to examine some of the theoretical approaches to curriculum planning. One of the earlier simplistic approaches was put forward by Tyler (1949) in his book *Basic Principles of Curriculum Instruction*. In the introduction, he identified four fundamental questions. These were:

1 What educational purposes should the school seek to attain?
2 What educational experiences can be provided that are likely to attain these purposes?
3 How can these educational experiences be effectively organized?
4 How can we determine whether these purposes are being attained?

The simple linear model which embraces aims and objectives, content, method and evaluation does not appear to take enough account of the inter-relationships between the defined elements. This particular limitation has prompted the suggestion that a cyclical model might be more appropriate (Taba 1962, Wheeler 1967, Nicholls and Nicholls 1972). This would allow the results of the evaluation to feed back to the original objectives to see if they have been achieved as well as to shape future courses. In theory, this represents a logical development and is usually referred to as 'rational curriculum planning'. There are, however, a number of disadvantages to such a process. One objection to the model is that it is a static representation of a dynamic and ever changing process and may lead to inflexibility by those who try to use it. For example, it may not always be necessary or appropriate to start with a precise definition of objectives. Another limitation is the suggestion that the evaluation component should be left to the end. In reality, all teachers are constantly making some kind of evaluation or judgement at every stage of the process. One of the dangers in examining the separate elements in detail is that the inter-relationships between them are ignored. Indeed, Kelly (1977) referred to the 'risk of serious distortion' by treating them separately and went on to suggest that the inter-relationship may well be one of 'the most important areas to be explored by curriculum theorists'.

A model which incorporates the same main components referred to above, but which gives greater flexibility, is the model proposed by Eraut *et al* (1975) and used at the University of Sussex for the analysis of curriculum materials (see *figure 1*).

Figure 1 Curriculum Model

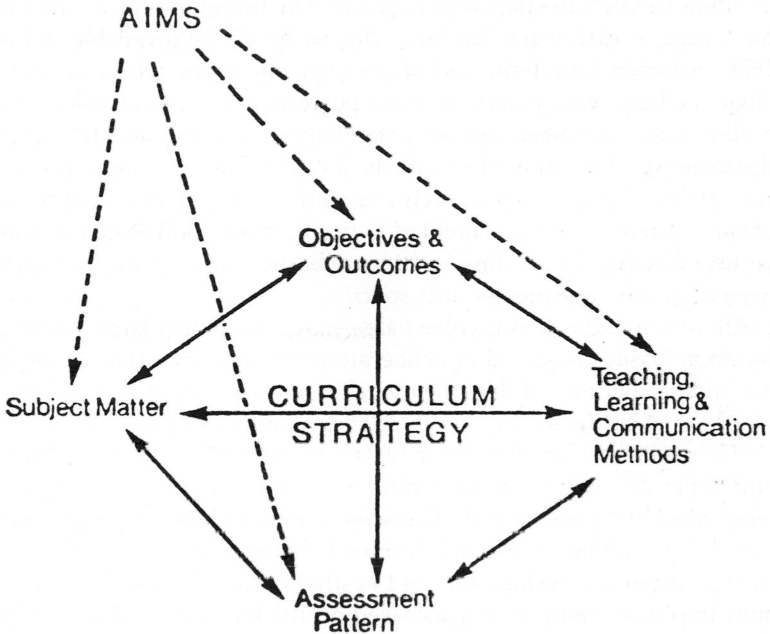

The aims of the subject form a background which influences all the main components of the planning. For example, the objectives will be derived from the aims, and the teaching methods adopted must be consistent with the overall aims. It is in this context that the rest of the planning takes place. The remaining components can then be arranged in any order and the whole process is therefore much more adaptable. Some teachers may begin with the content of the subject while others may start with teaching methods, the point of departure varying according to the needs of the class or the subject. This model would appear to be more adaptable than the narrower concept of rational curriculum planning and may be a closer representation of what is actually happening in schools. It appears to give teachers some flexibility in the way they plan their curriculum programmes. Whichever model is used as a framework, there is a common use of aims and objectives, content, method and evaluation, although the order and emphasis may vary. The importance and extent to which they are used in planning the physical education programme is at present pure conjecture. It would therefore seem appropriate at this stage to examine each of the main components in turn with a particular emphasis to physical education.

Aims and Objectives

The advisability of defining the aims and objectives of a course has been one of the most commonly debated issues in recent curriculum development. It is necessary to make a distinction between what is meant by aims and objectives, as there is often overlap and confusion in the literature about their precise meanings. A distinction has been drawn by Gibby (available in Lawton *et al* 1978) between long-term and short-term objectives when he stated, 'Broad aims, or long-term objectives, can be regarded as expressions of strategy, whilst short-term objectives are essentially tactical in character'. Linked to this distinction is the notion of specificity. In applying these definitions to physical education, a long-term goal such as moral development would be regarded as an aim, whereas the refinement of a specific motor skill would be considered to be an objective. Thus, aims are broad based and general in nature whereas objectives are very precise and specific.

All aims in education involve value judgements to a large extent because of the moral issues involved in deliberately setting out to change the behaviours of children. Because of this, the overall aims of a subject must be recognized as worthwhile by the society in which they operate. In physical education, Kane (1974) reviewed over 200 major texts and articles associated with the subject and suggested that there were nine main aims or long-term objectives which were most often mentioned. These were motor skills, self-realization, leisure, emotional stability, moral development, social competence, organic development, cognitive development and aesthetic appreciation. Kane's synopsis of aims in physical education was based on the literature and in a questionnaire, teachers were asked to rank the list presented to them. Whether or not the teachers of physical education would have chosen the same aims as Kane did, is open to question because they were not asked. A comparison of the results from these approaches would appear to be an interesting area of future investigation and this would involve talking to teachers about their own aims.

An examination of the aims listed above shows a range from the more overt areas of skill acquisition, leisure pursuits and organic fitness to the more covert aspects of aesthetic, moral and emotional development. The distinction between overt and covert aims is an important one in that it is much easier to specify objectives and evaluate results in the overt areas. For example, to give details of how long it should take to run 800 metres followed by a careful check of pulse rate recovery would be related to motor skills and organic development and could be stated in precise terms. To give a similar example from a covert aim such as moral development, specified in such exact detail, would be much more difficult. The danger is that this distinction may lead to an over-emphasis in the more easily identifiable aspects of the subject to the detriment of other equally important objectives. Whether or not teachers are adopting a narrow and objective approach to planning needs to be examined. In addition, the extent to which teachers communicate their aims and objectives to their pupils in any kind of structured way and whether more emphasis is placed on the overt areas is not clear.

Aims can, therefore, be broken down into objectives which are short-term in nature and part of the overall aim. However, their precise specification may not be quite so easy as might first appear. At least three criteria need to be observed in the structuring of objectives. First, they should be so specific that no room is left for doubt concerning the content and the context of the behaviour. An example might be the recognition of the important perceptual cues at the throw in from the goal line in netball. Even here, the importance of different cues would vary according to the skill level of the individual and would need to be specified. Secondly, the teacher needs to ensure that there is a hierarchy in the objectives and that progress is taking place. Trampolining would necessitate a sound grasp of the basic bounces before more advanced routines were attempted. Similarly in dance, technical ability is necessary to enhance the quality in creative movement. Thirdly, they should be broad based and cover objectives in the cognitive, motor skill and affective aspects. It is doubtful if all three criteria are observed by those teachers who do spell out their objectives in some detail. Some attempt may be made to satisfy the hierarchical requirement which is linked to progressive teaching, but it is questionable if the highly specific and broad-based criteria are followed. There is little evidence from any recent investigations to suggest that teachers plan in this way or any indication of the importance they attach to aims and objectives in the planning process.

The broad-based approach involving knowledge, motor skills and affective development is similar to the taxonomy of educational objectives by Bloom *et al* (1956 and 1964) which suggested a hierarchy of skills in the cognitive, affective and psycho-motor domains. Any suggestion that each domain is quite separate can be criticized and in, for example, the learning and performance of physical skills, it is impossible to isolate the physical from the cognitive and affective areas. All three domains are closely inter-related. Another criticism is that it is not always possible to agree on the precise placing of an objective in the taxonomy, and confusion can sometimes exist as to its exact position in the hierarchy. The fact that Bloom leaves the evaluation component to the last in the cognitive domain has been criticized by Lawton (1973), and he emphasizes the use of 'critical appraisal' at all stages of learning. With modern approaches to teaching in physical education, this is a particularly appropriate comment. For example, when problem-solving methods are used in the teaching of educational gymnastics, both the teacher and the children are making evaluative judgements from the beginning about the movement responses to the solutions of specific tasks. There is also a danger that a rigid following of Bloom's taxonomy in specifying intended learning outcomes might result in some of the more covert objectives in physical education being overlooked. Another problem is that knowledge may be made trivial through the demands for clarity and unambiguity in writing objectives. The number of objectives which could be written for any one course in physical education would be limitless and there is a danger they might become detached and unconnected.

Any suggestion that a long list of objectives could reflect the true nature of knowledge would be seriously questioned. Possibly the best use that can be made of the taxonomy may be to use the hierarchical structure as providing guidelines or check lists for the systematic preparation of objectives.

In applying the taxonomy to physical education, the importance of developing motor skills in a sporting context is one of the unique contributions the subject makes in education and hierarchical skill levels figure in many of the coaching manuals. In a consideration of the teachers' views of the extent to which involvement in physical education activities contributed to pupil effects, Kane's (1974) enquiry showed the four highest ranked effects were all in the affective domain, *viz:* enjoyment of participation, satisfaction from success, release from tension and general self-confidence, whereas cognitive judgements were moderately ranked. The prominence of the affective area is slightly surprising considering the essential nature of the physical element in physical education, and further evidence concerning these findings is necessary.

The model proposed by Eraut *et al* (1975) not only referred to objectives but also included outcomes. The reason for this combination may have been to allow objectives to cater for those aspects that can be identified and pre-specified, whereas outcomes may be unintended and cannot be specifically stated in such precise terms; this may be closer to the planning strategies adopted by physical education teachers. For example, in a swimming lesson objectives based on precise times and distances may have been scheduled, but there may be unexpected outcomes for some pupils related to confidence or an aesthetic appreciation of moving efficiently in water. In examining the concept of educational objectives, Eisner (1969) made a distinction between instructional objectives which are concerned with specifically identifying and defining the behaviour to be attained at the outset of the course, and expressive objectives which are not so specific, do not describe the terminal behaviour but refer instead to an 'educational encounter'. These alternatives are catered for by the use of the terms objectives and outcomes, and allow for spontaneous activity to take place as well as individual interpretation. Getting the right balance in the physical education curriculum between these two types of objectives is not easy and presents the teacher with a difficult task. At present, the extent to which members of the physical education profession make a distinction between objectives and outcomes in their planning procedures is not known.

Any plan which attempts to pre-specify objectives prior to the course beginning, is designing the curriculum by objectives and is most commonly referred to as the 'Objectives Model'. There have been a number of critics of this approach, notably, Eisner (1969), Stenhouse (1970 and 1975), Pring (1973) and Sockett (1976). Eisner does not wholly support the objectives approach and argues that some parts of the curriculum cannot be pre-specified. Thus he says, 'With an expressive objective what is desired is not homogeneity of response among students but diversity'. Thus, each individual personalizes his responses and this results in many different interpretations within a framework set by the teacher. In physical education, such an approach would be most meaningful, for example in such activities as dance, educational gymnastics and synchronized swimming, where there can be individual or group variation in the interpretation of music or a task set by the teacher. Apart from this major criticism, Stenhouse (1970) is concerned that the objectives model 'reduces content in education to an instrumental role'. In some areas of physical education, for example a group dance, participation in the activity might well be an experience in its own right and the benefits derived from it, such as social development, will be very personal and vary with the individual. A rigid pre-specification of objectives in these circumstances could be inappropriate.

There may often be a problem in measuring the attainment of some objectives, and it would be difficult to gather evidence to prove conclusively that a genuine change in behaviour had taken place in some of the covert areas. For example, the attainment of an ethical value in sport such as fair play may sometimes be enacted for the benefit of the teacher rather than an example of genuine learning. This would not be the case in an overt area such as fitness where strength and endurance levels can be measured through the use of objective tests.

Pring (1973) is also sceptical of the necessity for a prior statement of objectives in order to plan effectively on two main counts. First, because a precise specification of behaviour does not take into consideration the 'autonomous nature of the recipient'. Every pupil will make his own interpretation of each learning situation based on his own previous experiences. A good example would be the reactions of a class of pupils in a swimming pool which might range from acute anxiety to real enjoyment. Inevitably, this emotional involvement will affect individual interpretations. The second reason offered by Pring against the pre-specification of objectives is that, when dealing with children, one cannot 'pre-ordain what their final thoughts, judgements and evaluation would be'. Although this quotation referred to areas of social controversy in the Humanities Curriculum Project, it also has application in physical education. For example, in some of the covert aims of physical education, it may well prove difficult at the outset to state precisely the objectives we require our pupils to attain.

The narrow computer programming-type approach suggested by an objectives model leads to an over specification which can trivialize knowledge into low level and isolated knowledge and skills. This particular danger has been highlighted by Clegg (1975) when he warned of the dangers of overemphasizing an objectives approach in the pursuit of accountability. Clegg's comments were based on his observation of trends in education in the USA, where in some states, objective tests have been devised to measure most aspects of pupil learning. If this trend was to be followed in the planning of physical education in this country, it would require objectives to be defined in clear and unambiguous terms and the extent to which they had been achieved would have to be measured. At present, there is no evidence to indicate whether or not physical education curriculum planning in this country is moving in this direction.

Although some curriculum theorists argue strongly for the pre-specification of objectives, Taylor (1970) has provided some evidence that teachers may well begin their planning from a different and more practical starting point. This alternative was concerned with the interests and abilities of pupils, and with subject matter. In Taylor's study, eighty academic subject syllabuses were analyzed by three independent judges who decided the proportion of each syllabus devoted to aims and objectives, content, method and evaluation. In all subjects, content received the largest proportion and evaluation the least. Although the results can only be taken as a general guide, the content of the subject does appear to have the greatest emphasis in the written syllabus. A similar analysis is not available in the physical education literature and only tentative interpretations can be made at present. Further support for alternative starting points is also provided by Zahorik (1975) who analyzed the methods of planning of 194 teachers and found that the decision they most frequently made first was concerned with content. These indications are contrary to the notion of starting with a pre-specification of objectives in planning. What is not clear is whether the same trends are apparent in physical education. If they are, then the objectives mdoel does not accurately reflect what is happening in schools.

In spite of these criticisms, no-one would suggest that there should be no planning at all. Formulating objectives has the advantage that it can provide direction to teaching and Davies (1976) supported this by saying, 'To deny the usefulness of objectives is to cast the teachers into the role of opportunists and entrepreneurs in all their dealings'. Good teaching is often linked to good planning and in some cases this may best be done through an initial specification of objectives. This prior specification has the effect of making the teacher plan in precise terms rather than vague ideals for individual lessons or a course of work. If objectives are given to the children prior to starting a block of work, this can provide a sense of direction as well as motivating the children to achieve. The extent to which physical education teachers communicate their objectives to children is not known and information in this area would provide an important link in the planning process.

When objectives are clearly stated in written form, they can be used as a starting point for the evaluation process. For example, an objective related to knowledge of the laws or rules of a game could be evaluated through efficiency of officiating or a paper and pencil test, whereas an objective concerned with social development might be evaluated through teacher observation. The extent to which teachers of physical education systematically attempt to evaluate their original aims through their objectives is not clear. Nor is there any firm evidence about the part played by evaluation in the planning of future courses. The importance of these processes is strongly argued by the advocates of an objectives approach, but the extent of their use in physical education planning is not known.

It would appear that an objectives model and the ideas behind rational curriculum planning are too dogmatic and prescriptive to be applicable to all the planning in physical education. They may have most value in the more overt areas of the subject as well as in what Poulton (1957) referred to as 'closed' skills in which the motor requirements are predictable and there is little reliance on the external environment. Skills such as shot-putting and diving would be examples from this classification. Approaches which do not initially pre-specify their objectives can also be valuable and the issue would seem to revolve round the concept of 'appropriateness'. Thus, a variety of approaches may not only be most valuable, but also reflect practice in schools. Although aims and objectives are important components of planning, the other areas of content, method and evaluation are also at the heart of curriculum planning and it is the order, emphasis and inter-relationship that is given to each aspect which is critical.

Irrespective of whether the aims and objectives have to be pre-specified or not, the attainment of intended learning outcomes has to be achieved through the teaching of those practical areas which comprise physical education. These reflect the content of the subject and is the next main area to be considered.

Content

Some evidence has already been cited in the previous section which suggested that teachers may not only give content the largest weighting in their planning, but also start their planning by a detailed consideration of this aspect. One of the reasons why this may happen in physical education is because there is a great deal of information available in the literature. The Governing Bodies of sport (*eg.* Rugby and Cricket) provide coaching manuals and progressive schemes of work which can readily be used by teachers in their planning. Another reason may be that content is a very tangible starting point and one with which teachers can identify.

The subject matter in the secondary school will usually be a selection from the six main areas of athletics, dance, games, gymnastics, swimming and outdoor pursuits. This is substantiated by Whitehead and Hendry (1976) who used a questionnaire to elicit information about the physical education curriculum in schools from 196 teachers in the north of England. The curriculum that emerged from this study showed a limited range of activities in operation (similar to those outlined by Kane in 1974) and concluded that, 'the content of secondary schools' physical education programmes for boys and girls seems not to have changed as radically as many may have believed'. Thus, in spite of recent changes in educational thought and practice, and changes in the length and content of teacher education, the content in schools appears to have remained remarkably stable over quite a long period.

The allocation of curriculum time to any one practical area will be dependent on a number of variables such as the stage of schooling, the needs of the children and the organization within the school. The nature of the geographical area, the facilities and abilities of the staff will also shape the programme that is offered. In addition, there is likely to be some variation between the boys' and the girls' curriculum. Whatever the variables, and these will differ from school to school, decisions have to be made prior to the academic year about what is to be attempted and in which terms of the school year. The decisions that are mde can be recorded in the written physical education syllabus. If the content is presented in this way, it allows for a detailed analysis to be made concerning the amount of time devoted to each subject area in each term.

In the first two or three years of the secondary school curriculum, it should be possible to be quite precise about the total time allocation that is devoted to athletics, dance, games, gymnastics, swimming and outdoor pursuits. On the basis of this analysis, a number of questions can be posed. For example, how many hours are devoted to gymnastics in the first two years? Does one area of the subject have an excessive time allocation? Are other areas neglected? One of the dangers in physical education is that it is becoming so diversified that children are allowed, and in some cases encouraged, to participate in a wide range of activities. This diversity mitigates against any activity being taken to any real depth of study and understanding. An analysis of the curriculum time allocation would appear to be a useful first stage in planning, but the extent to which a 'time analysis' is used by teachers is not known.

The majority of schools offer a basic core of work, chosen from the six main practical areas, during the first three years of secondary education (Kane 1974). However, the trend is one of decreased compulsion and increased choice of options the longer the pupil remains in school. When choices are offered, they should, wherever possible, be based on a substantial core of work and this then enables a child to make an informed choice. Through his own experience he should know those activities in which he shows some aptitude and which appeal to him. Thus an opportunity for some specialization is presented and this is in contrast to haphazard diversity of choice. One of the aims of every teacher should be to try to enable all children to reach their optimum potential and this is one way in which direction and guidance can be given. Whether or not there should be total specialization in one activity is open to question. To achieve sporting excellence in modern society requires total dedication and many hours spent in training. Within the physical education curriculum there should perhaps be some 'guided' choice. McIntosh (1963) suggested a classification which divided physical activities into combat, competitive, conquest and expressive groupings. Many other categories are possible such as indoor and outdoor, individual, team and racket games. However, a choice of activities from a comparatively small number of categories is probably most realistic, although once a choice has been made, some consideration should be given to the range of choices to make certain that a balance is maintained between the activities. This would ensure, for example, that the activities chosen were not all individual in nature and that some co-operative activities were included. Regardless of whether an activity is part of the common core of work or an optional activity, it is incumbent on every teacher to plan all courses with the same care and attention to detail. Personal observation in a few schools would suggest that there may be some optional activities where children are left to their own devices without any form of guidance or instruction whatsoever. This kind of planning is not acceptable and the extent of this practice warrants some investigation.

An essential feature of good planning is that the experiences that are offered to the children should be progressive in nature. This can happen in two broad ways. First, in a vertical fashion within the subject, where the work of one term or year is used as a basis for future development, and second, in a horizontal manner, where links are made with other aspects of physical education or with other subjects in the curriculum. It is possible to plan for links within the subject through, for example, the use of common themes in gymnastics and dance, and principles of play within the variety of games that are offered. The establishment of links with other subjects does, however, require much more preparation and consultation. For example, the ability of children to observe, analyze and judge is not the sole prerogative of physical education and could well be a claim made by science education. This suggests that subjects should not work in separate compartments but that some kind of inter-relationship should exist and that objectives in one area could be complemented in another. The study by Kane (1974) indicated that nearly two-thirds of the departments in a one-in-ten sample of secondary schools in England and Wales were involved in such inter-disciplinary studies at least to some extent. This suggests that some collaboration is taking place between departments in schools who use this approach. However, the exact nature of these integrated studies is not specified. The Keele Integrated Studies Project (1973) defined integration as 'the exploration of any large area, theme or problem which a) requires the help of more than one subject discipline for its full understanding, and b) is best taught by the concerted action of a team of teachers'. There are many topic areas that could well be investigated in this way. For example, 'Sport and Society' could lead to a study of the many aspects of sport and recreation in local areas and society at large, while 'Mechanics of Movement' would inevitably link science with a variety of running, striking, throwing and jumping activities. A topic based on the Olympics could lead to political, historical, ethical as well as physical and scientific considerations. One report which did refer to such an integrated approach was reported by Armstrong (1976) in which 'Human Movement' contained physiological and psychological perspectives, and 'Sport, Leisure and Society' used a more sociological approach. At present, there appears to be little available evidence to suggest that integrated projects such as those outlined above are actually being taught in schools. The same lack of evidence is also apparent concerning the extent to which links are used within the subject.

A number of issues have been highlighted in the planning of the content of the physical education curriculum about which there is a dearth of information. These issues relate to the use made by teachers of a 'time analysis' of the various activities, the relationship between, and the amount of planning devoted to, the common core and optional activities, and the amount and type of integration that takes place within the subject. All these factors are important variables, and the extent to which they form part of the planning procedures of practising teachers warrants further enquiry.

Whatever decision is made concerning the content to be included in the curriculum, the activities have to be taught to the pupils and a variety of teaching methods are available. A consideration of these methods is the next main area to be examined.

Teaching Method

In their review of research on teaching physical education, Nixon and Locke (1973) stated, 'It is probable that relatively few decisions about teaching, as distinct from the curriculum, are made until the class is under way'. This suggests that teachers adopt a rather haphazard approach, and while an element of spontaneity is an essential ingredient in all good teaching, for optimum efficiency, suitable teaching strategies should be planned before the lesson.

All plans have to be implemented at some stage, and in physical education, these will take place in the gymnasium, the swimming pool or the outdoor environment. There has been a great deal of research in the psychological area of motor learning (for example, Lawther 1968, Cratty 1973 and Singer 1975) which has provided some helpful guidelines to the profession. However, much of this work has been related to such isolated variables as motivation, practice and transfer of training in well controlled experimental situations. In physical education, the implementation of any plan takes place during the actual lesson and it is somewhat surprising that there has been comparatively little research on this part of the curriculum process in physical education. Inevitably, the teaching method that is adopted by a teacher will depend upon a number of variables such as the children being taught and the specific nature of the activity.

A number of distinct teaching styles have been identified by Mosston (1972) and the choice of an appropriate style for particular teaching situations is important. For example, at certain stages in the acquisition of skills, where a prescribed standard is laid down, a directed form of teaching may be most appropriate. In contrast, a creative approach may be more suited where tasks are open to individual interpretation in gymnastics and dance. Mosston has proposed a spectrum of teaching styles which are integrally connected. The names he gives to each style are: Command, Task, Reciprocal, Individual Programme-Teacher's Design, Guided Discovery, Problem Solving, and Individual Programme-Student's Design. Each style merges into the next and offers a range of alternatives to the teacher in his approach to the teaching situation. Mosston goes on to consider the contribution each style can make to the physical, social, emotional and intellectual development of the child. The analysis provides a valuable theoretical framework for teaching which can be used as a guideline by the teacher to help him develop his own unique teaching patterns. Every teacher needs a wide range of skills available in his repertoire which enables him to vary his teaching and avoid a stereotyped approach. The ability to use different teaching skills effectively should enable teachers to present their work in a manner which allows the children the opportunity to learn to the best of their ability.

Linked to the particular teaching style that a teacher adopts are the prior decisions which have to be made about the analysis and presentation of the materials and skills. Most current work in the field of information processing in motor skills (as considered by Whiting 1969, Gentile 1972 and Marteniuk 1976) emphasizes the necessity of identifying pertinent cues and communicating these to the learner so that ambiguity or confusion is reduced to a minimum. The amount and type of information that is presented will, of course, vary according to the skill level of the performer. Some children are more easily able to visualize what is required of them through verbal communication, whilst others prefer visual guidance. Some prefer a more directed approach in contrast to those who enjoy the freedom to approach a problem in their own way. The analysis of each skill and its presentation would thus seem to be important if the individual nature of the learning is taken into consideration.

The importance of a complete analysis of the teaching and learning process has been advocated by Singer and Dick (1974) through their development of a systems approach to teaching. In this system, broad instructional goals are identified at the outset and this is followed by a detailed analysis of the skill and the performer before more precise objectives are formulated. The next stage emphasizes the importance of criterion-referenced evaluation and this 'takes into account the direct relationship between the design of the evaluation instrument and the statement of the performance objective'. Thus, the evaluation is directly linked to the objectives of the course. Once this has been decided, then the instructional strategies are planned. Evaluation takes place at the end about the effectiveness of the teaching and the extent to which objectives have been achieved. This in turn provides feedback to the pupil about his progress and to the teacher about his teaching. This system has many similarities to the rational curriculum planning model and the sequential order in which each phase is planned. The application of this approach to physical education is possible and these authors give several detailed examples how this may be achieved. It is probable that few teachers actually plan in this way. However, this is not to say that teachers should not be encouraged to plan along these guidelines when it is considered to be appropriate.

The nature of the activity and the objectives to be taught will also have an influence on the teaching methods to be adopted. In addition, there is no doubt that some instructional methods are better than others in achieving certain objectives. For example, in the teaching of techniques in dance, the teacher may decide that the most appropriate place to operate is where he can exercise a high degree of authority and direct the teaching. At a later stage, when interpretation and creative ideas are called for, much greater freedom will be given to the children. In contrast, a different profile may result in the case of swimming. Using artificial aids and a multistroke approach, considerable freedom to experiment may be offered to the children initially. This could be followed by a more directed situation involving stroke technique, until finally children are asked to choose group work, create synchronized swims and prepare their own schedules of work. Different aspects of the physical education programme may best be taught by the use of a variety of teaching styles. The Schools Council Enquiry by Kane (1974) asked physical education teachers to indicate the frequency with which they used teaching styles described as direct, guided discovery, problem-solving, creative and individualized programmes. It is important to note that they were asked to consider the programme as a whole rather than any one specific part. However, the extent to which teachers are able to make accurate and reliable judgements about their own teaching styles could be questioned, as it is not easy to make this type of self-analysis. Indeed, there are many occasions when a variety of styles are used in the same lesson or course of study. Consequently, the results can only be regarded as general trends. The responses from the teachers in Kane's study indicated that creative and individualized programmes were ranked lowest for both men and women teachers. Women teachers gave most emphasis to guided discovery, followed by problem-solving styles with direct teaching rated third. This contrasted with the men teachers who used a directed style most frequently followed by guided discovery and problem-solving styles in that order. In commenting on this difference, Kane suggested that women teachers were 'less committed to styles of teaching which require them to pre-determine and directly control the learning sequence, and being more committed to styles which involve the pupils seeking solutions'. Whether male teachers do in fact give greater stress to the specification of objectives is not entirely clear and warrants further investigation. Differences were also revealed in the study related to age, with younger teachers emphasizing guided discovery and problem-solving styles significantly more and direct teaching significantly less than older teachers. The reason for these differences is not apparent from the data but may be partly explained by the different nature of the subject content. For example, the gymnastics that is taught by men and women in secondary schools ranges from the formal skills of Olympic gymnastics to the individual interpretation of tasks in educational gymnastics and the subject content would, to some extent, determine the style of approach. Whether or not younger teachers give a greater emphasis to educational gymnastics is not known but this suggestion could form the basis of a tentative interpretation.

The interpretation from this part of Kane's study gives an overall impression based upon teachers' assessments of their own teaching styles. It would also be advantageous to have an independent observer to analyze an individual lesson or series of lessons to see if the teaching style is consistent with the short-term objectives. Analysis of a specific lesson in physical education can be justified in that the teacher deliberately sets out with the intention that children shall learn either motor skills, attitudes or knowledge and this necessitates a change in behaviour. Inevitably, moral issues tend to be involved. In the present climate of accountability, it is essential that there are techniques available that can be used by teachers to evaluate the effectiveness of their lessons. There are several interaction analysis systems which allow a more detailed examination of the verbal behaviour of the teacher and pupil. The most notable system is the one developed by Flanders (1970) which allows recordings of dominant behaviour to be recorded every three seconds in ten pre-defined categories. A number of systems have been specifically developed for physical education (for example, Cheffers, 1972, Heinilä, 1979 and Tavecchio, 1977), but such systems tend to be rather sophisticated, requiring a great deal of training in order to become familiar with the recording procedures and they often need a computer for analysis. What is also needed is a simplified procedure which can be used by teachers to analyze the verbal behaviour and the physical movements of an individual, a group or a class of children in a variety of physical education settings.

Over the past decade, a number of elaborate systems of analysis have been developed at Teachers' College, Columbia University. Details of this work, entitled the Videotape Data Bank Project, have recently been reported by Anderson and Barrette (1978). The project has developed a number of complementary systems which examine different aspects of the physical education lesson in the USA. Their main findings were reviewed by Hurwitz (1978) who identified three major themes. The first deals with the remarkably rapid pace and constant change in the lesson, the second theme identified a traditional teacher-centred approach, and lastly, there was considerable variation between classes in the communication patterns used by the teachers and the pupils. There is a need to replicate the work of this project in other countries. Whilst there are many interesting results, we should apply them to our own culture with caution. For example, the finding that the predominant mode of teaching was directed in nature is unexpected when one considers the emphasis that has been given to individual development in education. In addition, there was almost a complete absence of educational gymnastics and dance lessons and a selection of teaching in this country which did not include a substantial proportion of these types of lessons would reflect a biased sample. Whether or not an analysis of a range of activities in our own culture would produce similar findings is worthy of investigation, but an extensive survey is beyond the scope of this book. Information which is pertinent to our own teaching profession is more likely to have greater impact on the teacher than 'imported' data. The analysis techniques used in the project were quite sophisticated and mainly for use by researchers. What is needed, for teacher use, is the development of a simplified system or systems for recording the physical and verbal behaviour of the teacher and pupils in a variety of physical education settings and this has been attempted by Underwood (1978 and 1980).

There is no doubt that a variety of teaching methods can be used by physical education teachers and they have considerable autonomy in the manner in which they conduct their lessons. However, the emphasis teachers give to teaching method in their planning is not clear, and there is some indication that it may be a slightly neglected area. In addition, there appears to be a dearth of methods for use by physical education teachers which will enable them to examine the effectiveness of particular teaching strategies. This type of analysis is inevitably linked with evaluation procedures which is the next section to be considered.

Evaluation

In physical education, the term evaluation is often linked with tests and measurements and it is important to be clear exactly what is meant by these terms. A test, in the narrowest sense, is just a number of questions to be answered or physical skills to be performed, and, as a result of a pupil's performance in the test, a measurement is made which could give an assessment of the level of achievement in that activity or of any change that might have taken place. In physical education, it is possible to quantify many performances by reference to external standards such as time, distance or fitness norms, but its overall value cannot be established merely by this quantification. In contrast to this objective approach, many of the measurements made by the teacher about his own teaching are through his own observation of lessons or pupils. The term evaluation is broader than assessment and is concerned with determining the value of something. This is supported by Taylor (1976) who remarked that, 'No amount of measurement, only valuing can indicate what is worthwhile'. Such valuing will inevitably be influenced by the personal preferences and standards of the teacher. In theory, evaluation should provide both quantitative and qualitative information about the process and the product in physical education which, in turn, can be used to improve future teaching and planning. It is therefore necessary to consider evaluation taking place at every stage of the educational process and quite wrong to think of it only taking place at the end.

This all-embracing notion of evaluation attempts to throw light on all stages of the curriculum process. Parlett and Hamilton wrote a paper entitled *Evaluation as Illumination* (available in Tawney, 1976) and drew a distinction between the classical or 'agricultural-botany' model which relied upon a psychometric approach and examined whether or not certain pre-specified objectives had been obtained, and illuminative evaluation which is 'rooted in social anthropology, seeks rather to describe and interpret, and takes account of the contexts in which educational innovation must function. Central concepts are the instructional system and the learning *milieu*'. Thus the classical evaluation had focussed on the end results and paid little attention to the process involved. The polarity of these approaches suggests that there may be a danger of favouring one method to the exclusion of another, and that there is a cleavage between qualitative and quantitative approaches. Both Lawton (1978), and Smith and Fraser (1980), argue for the use of a variety of methods and suggest that an eclectic approach can enhance evaluation. Choosing the most appropriate method or methods to gather data from which an evaluation can be made would seem to be sound common sense. This may be sensible and logical in theory, but it is a very time consuming process. The ways in which physical education teachers judge the success of their curriculum planning has not been investigated in depth. Whether greater emphasis is given to the evaluation of motor skills (which are mainly measured quantitatively) or the evaluation of affective aspects (which are mainly measured qualitatively) is speculative at present.

One of the drawbacks of the so called 'classical evaluation' was the reliance upon samples large enough to warrant statements concerning statistical significance. Eisner (1979) expressed unease with current evaluation techniques and referred to an essential difference between 'statistical and educational significance'. In his view, it is not always necessary to have large samples before inferences can be made, and he advocates the use of language as well as making a plea for teachers to be literate in the tools of curriculum evaluation. This wider approach has also been advocated by Cope (1975) who considered that teachers require many evaluative and assessment skills from 'simple measurement to complex observation, and to formal and informal discussion with colleagues, and, very important, with pupils'. This type of evaluation encompasses both empirical and humanistic evaluation, but there is no documentary evidence available to suggest the extent to which they are being used in schools.

In relation to the use made by physical education teachers of written comments in the evaluation of pupils, many secondary school reports have restricted space (often one line) available which makes it impossible to write detailed comments. There is, however, a trend towards a more open and unrestricted form of reporting which would at least allow fuller comments to be made about pupils' progress.

It has been suggested by Luff (1980) that curriculum evaluation is a rather neglected process in physical education and she advocates an 'illuminative' approach. She suggests that greater use needs to be made of formative evaluation which will give the teacher current feedback about instructional methods. Apart from the day-to-day evaluation that most teachers conduct, there have been remarkably few systematic studies in this area of physical education. One study which is worthy of comment was conducted by Carroll (1976). He carried out a number of open-ended interviews with physical education teachers in an attempt to establish their criteria for the evaluation of individual lessons. The main criteria he established were related to: attainment; teaching-presentation; exercise value; behaviour of pupils; pupils' enjoyment; effort and interest. In commenting on the results of his interviews, Carroll stated, 'low attainment is acceptable as long as effort is high'. Whether such a statement reflects the attitude of all physical education teachers needs to be verified. In addition, in view of the fact that physical education makes a unique contribution to the physical fitness of a pupil, the importance of this aspect to the evaluation process needs probing. There is also a noticeable absence of social, moral and aesthetic objectives in the list which had figured prominently in Kane's earlier study. This suggests that there may be a discrepancy between the theorists' and teachers' objectives and this warrants examination. In addition, the extent to which teachers systematically evaluate their original aims and objectives also needs investigating.

If evaluation is to be an integral part of curriculum planning, then it has to be largely based in schools if it is to be relevant and effective. The idea of school-based evaluation with the 'Teacher as Researcher' has been suggested by a number of writers, as for example by Pring (available in Lawton *et al* 1978). It is not suggested that the teacher should carry out empirical studies with large groups but should do what Pring suggests which is 'to think systematically and critically about what he is doing'. This is in relation to the teachers' planning and teaching of courses as well as evaluating pupil achievements. In this type of evaluation, the emphasis is on self-evaluation which is particularly difficult for a teacher who is centrally involved in the planning and execution of the curriculum. Pring goes on to suggest six test procedures which might be used. The first is the use of an interaction analysis schedule which enables the behaviour of the teacher and pupil to be placed into pre-specified categories. This technique gives detailed information about a teaching situation and makes a vital link between any objectives that might have been stated and the end results. The technique does attempt to examine the process of teaching and can suggest or confirm courses of action for the future. The main value will lie in the fact that 'real life' data will be available to the teacher about his own teaching style. Clearly, the development of an interaction analysis system capable of being used by teachers might well be a useful addition to physical education evaluation techniques.

The second is the use of a participant observer who would provide a different and objective account of the same lesson. The use of the term 'critical friend' would be an apt description of the role such a person would play. However, it is important to note that the observation and criticism, however constructive, of a teacher's lesson will be a sensitive area and a suitable climate has to be established before any worthwhile work can develop. The most difficult problem will be to find a suitable person to observe and comment on a lesson, but there are occasions in team teaching or when students are on teaching practice when this might be possible.

Recording is the third test procedure suggested. The use of a tape recorder would allow a teacher to listen to his own voice and enable him to make an evaluation about such aspects of teaching as the clarity of his communication and the use of praise in feedback to the class or individual pupils. The use of videotape recording would add a different dimension to the analysis and is used in some schools. The linking of videotapes with interaction analysis schedules might be an even more rewarding area of development.

Pring's fourth suggestion is for the teacher to keep first hand reports. Although these may give a biased account, they would provide information about a course which might be helpful in future decision-making. Where courses are taught by more than one member of staff, the use of a departmental book to record each teacher's impressions would be useful for the purposes of comparison. Innovatory planning such as the extension of an options programme in physical education would have the benefit of two independently written reports which would be helpful in any summative evaluation of the course.

The fifth procedure suggests that the perceptions other people have of a lesson can often be different from the one formed by the teacher. In schools, a teacher researcher would have to ask the pupils their reactions to a lesson or programme of work. Apart from casual conversation with pupils, there is little evidence to suggest that this is a technique used by physical education teachers.

Finally Pring refers to triangulation. This is a method which involves three separate accounts of a tape recorded lesson from the teacher, an observer and the children. Comparisons can then be made which provide very real starting points for discussion. In this approach, the children are asked, in confidence, what they consider a lesson or course has achieved. This method was developed in the Ford Teaching Project (1975) and established a strong link between the researchers and teachers who were actively teaching in schools.

At present, most teachers of physical education probably do not have the necessary understanding or experience to use many of these techniques effectively in schools, and even if they did, many would say that they do not have the time to evaluate in this way. However, perhaps teachers should devote more time to evaluating their own work. Future developments could certainly concentrate on co-operative research between the specialists in the field of education and the practising teacher. This would go some way to achieving MacDonald and Walker's (1975) ideal when they stated, 'The real prize is the prospect of developing techniques and procedures which can be used by schools and ancillary agencies. A specialist research profession will always be a poor substitute for a self-monitoring educational community'. The ideals expressed in this quotation are certainly some way from being realized in the physical education profession, mainly because suitable techniques and qualified researchers are not readily available. No matter which kinds of evaluation are used, they should act as a type of feedback to the planning process. Wilhelms (1971) suggested that any system of evaluation should meet some basic criteria, and four of these are particularly appropriate to physical education. The first is that it should facilitate self-evaluation. This is concerned with the learner being able to assess his own ability and potential in a variety of physical situations and being able to build self concepts. In addition, the teacher should be able to make an accurate evaluation of his own teaching and the curriculum programme. Secondly, it should incorporate every objective valued by the school. This would encompass development in physical prowess, knowledge and attitudes. Thirdly, it must facilitate learning and teaching. Every aspect of any evaluative information should give an indication of the effectiveness of present work and a guide to future planning. Lastly, it must produce appropriate records for every child. This should not only be a record of achievement in school teams by the more able, but should also make reference to the attitude, contribution and personal development of each individual.

Emerging Issues

The review has examined four main aspects of curriculum planning *viz:* aims and objectives, content, method and evaluation and discussed each one in relation to physical education. Although each main aspect has been considered separately it would be wrong to assume that each one is self-contained. Curriculum planning should be regarded as a whole and not a piecemeal activity. The inter-relationships and emphases that occur in planning will vary from school to school and from teacher to teacher but the eventual outcome must reflect a fully integrated approach.

Further, the review of literature has identified a number of studies which have some bearing on planning in physical education. Some of these studies relate to the general principles of planning, others refer to academic subjects and the remainder to isolated aspects of physical education. In terms of curriculum research, physical education appears to be comparatively untouched in this country. Even the Schools Council Enquiry was merely an attempt to identify current trends and practices in schools and was only seen as a first stage in curriculum development. However, one aspect which was revealed from this enquiry was that teachers would welcome some guidance in their curriculum planning. It, therefore, seems appropriate that some attempt should be made to unify the available evidence and collect new evidence concerning the totality of planning a complete physical education curriculum.

Whatever limitations some of the curriculum planning models may have, the relationship between, and the emphasis given to the main components of aims and objectives, content, method and evaluation are important if logical development is to take place. In the literature review, so far, it has been suggested that there are a number of ways in which planning can be carried out and that it is not always necessary, or indeed advisable, to start with a statement of objectives. The weighting which physical education teachers give to each of the components in their planning is not known. In addition, there is an indication that the sex and age of the teacher may be important variables in the emphasis which they give to the different aspects. This points to the uniqueness of planning and suggests that it may be more appropriate to consider guiding principles rather than attempt to be prescriptive.

The aims of any subject will inevitably underpin much of the planning which takes place. The precise aims of physical education may not be entirely clear as there is an indication that some of the aims identified by the theorists are not recognized by practising teachers. In addition, there may be age and sex differences between teachers concerning the importance of particular aims. Partly because of this slightly confused position, the extent to which teachers communicate their aims, and, where appropriate, their objectives to the pupils they teach in any systematic way is not clear. It would seem reasonable that the main purposes of the subject, or course, should be conveyed to children and this might well be a useful strategy if used more frequently by members of the physical education profession.

Nearly all schools appear to operate a common core of work in the first few years of secondary education, with an options programme being given a greater proportion of time in each successive year. The relationship of activities within and between the common core and the options programme needs to be analyzed to ensure that a balanced programme is put into operation. There is some suggestion that the optional activities programme in some schools may be a 'soft option'. By this is meant that children may be placed into activities of their choice and allowed to participate with little or no guidance and instruction. This would infer that teachers spend less time in the planning and preparation of the optional activities programme than they do for the common core activities. Whether this is the case is not clear.

Another area in which there is little information concerns the number of links that teachers attempt to make within the subject. This applies to progression within the same practical areas from year to year, as well as the links that are made between the differing activities in physical education. Planned progressions and links within the subject can only lead to a more efficient presentation, but the extent of their use is not clear at present. Because of the different activities involved in physical education, there may be a tendency for teachers to regard them as being in separate compartments rather than them all contributing to an integrated whole.

Another issue which has emerged is the need to be able to analyze, in a comparatively simple and straightforward manner, the teaching situation, and the literature review identified three main trends. The first trend is that there appears to be little research on physical education in natural settings, which is surprising when one considers that the implementation of any plan can only take place between the teacher and the children during the actual lesson. Regardless of the quality of syllabus presentation, or the breakdown of aims into objectives, the 'transaction phase' is a vital link in effective planning. Secondly, there are few objective methods for classifying the actions of both teacher and pupil in a physical education lesson which can be used by the teacher with the help of a colleague. The third trend emphasized the importance of developing the 'Teacher as Researcher' in relation to his planning and teaching. Interaction analysis was suggested as one method by which the teacher could examine the process of his teaching, as well as investigate the links between objectives and end results. This type of analysis would produce data pertinent to a particular lesson and assist the teacher in making judgements about the effectiveness of his own teaching strategies.

The role played by evaluation in the theoretical approaches is a vital one, both in respect of the part it plays in the planning of future courses as well as evaluating the original aims of the subject. Whether physical education teachers attach the same importance to evaluation, and use it for these specific purposes, is speculative at present. In addition, the ways in which teachers judge the success of their courses, and whether they give greater emphasis to the evaluation of overt to the exclusion of covert aims is by no means clear. No doubt there are a number of individual differences in the way this is approached, but it should be possible to identify some underlying criteria.

Planning cannot be the sole prerogative of the head of department, and it must be the result of the combined efforts of all the staff. The extent to which staff are involved in this planning, and when and how it takes place, has not been investigated. Presumably, there will be a variety of factors which will influence curriculum planning and these will vary from school to school. However, there may be some factors which are common to all schools regardless of their geographical location or type or size of school.

One area in which there has been substantial development in recent years has been in the submission of CSE programmes in physical education. These courses take place during Years 4 and 5, and usually a minimum time allocation of four single periods is required. Carroll (1981) has indicated that the number of schools submitting CSE courses has nearly doubled during the last four years. Most are Mode III submissions which involve the school in the preparation of the syllabus and the assessment of the course. The regional Boards then appoint moderators to advise them on the syllabus content and standards of assessment. Some standardization is now taking place with the increase of Mode I submissions where the syllabus and assessment are external to the school. The preparation and presentation of CSE courses is a time-consuming process and 'most Boards insist on a list of objectives which are attainable through the examination' (Carroll 1981). Perhaps without realizing it, teachers found this approach helpful since it required them to present structured programmes, which had objectives, content and evaluation.

Most of the discussion has centred around the secondary school curriculum and the decision to conduct this study in this age range is made for two reasons. The first arises from the statement by Kane (1974) in *Physical Education in Secondary Schools* that teachers would welcome help and advice in the planning of the curriculum and it seems appropriate that some attempt should be made to produce some material which might answer this need. The second reason is that all the teaching experience and study of the author has been in secondary schools or colleges of education which trained students to teach in secondary education. It is hoped that this experience will enable insight to be brought to the problems that arise.

At present, hard evidence about planning procedures is not available. This lack of knowledge points to the necessity and importance of a detailed examination of the planning and implementation of the physical education curriculum in the secondary school, and this study investigates the central role played by teachers in this process.

2 The Physical Education Curriculum: School-Based Research

The purpose of the investigation was to examine ways in which teachers of physical education plan, carry out and evaluate their secondary school courses in physical education. In particular, the study attempted to investigate:

1 how teachers plan and implement their curriculum with special reference to aims and objectives, content, teaching methods and evaluation;
2 which factors influence the main components of curriculum planning.

As indicated in the last chapter, the review of literature revealed many issues that warranted further examination. It was not possible to examine them all so it was decided to focus the research strategy on the behaviour of the teacher and the ways in which he planned and implemented the physical education curriculum. This decision was made because the teacher is central to the planning process and it is around him that most of the issues will revolve. In particular, the head of a physical education department plays a bigger role than his colleagues in planning and, wherever possible, departmental heads were consulted. Because of this emphasis, it meant that other issues, such as the part played by the pupils in certain aspects of planning, did not form a major part of the investigation. Although recognizing the importance of such issues, it was decided to focus on teacher behaviour in planning.

In an attempt to obtain a variety of perspectives on the issues to be investigated, it was felt advisable to use more than one type of research strategy. A single research approach, such as a questionnaire or observation techniques would have given only a limited perspective and not provided enough insight into the issues to be examined. Three appropriate methods for collecting data for the proposed investigation could be, as Moser and Kalton (1979) have suggested, interviewing the people concerned, examining documentary sources and the use of a mailed questionnaire. Each one of these methods was considered appropriate for use in this study and those used in the initial stages helped to shape future developments. The three main research strategies used were:

1 *Interviews with teachers* The heart of curriculum planning in physical educa-

tion lies in the schools and needs to be undertaken by teachers who are actively engaged in teaching the subject. It therefore seemed sensible to begin at the 'grass roots' level and talk to teachers. The responsibility for planning is held by the heads of department and the discussions with them focussed on their planning procedures.

2 *Examining physical education syllabuses* The planning of a syllabus of work is part of the professional responsibility of every teacher and all schools should have a written syllabus available. An analysis of their format and the emphasis they gave to the main components of planning presented a different perspective to the investigation.

3 *The Questionnaire* So far, the research strategies have been conducted with comparatively small numbers. The smallness of each sample was mainly due to the time-consuming nature of the approaches being used. A questionnaire was therefore distributed throughout secondary schools in England and Wales in order to widen the scope of the study and allow a fuller investigation of some of the major questions and issues that had earlier been claimed worthy of attention.

Each of the above strategies was conducted separately and enabled information to be collected from a variety of sources using different methods. However, the results which emerged from the investigations were examined, compared and interrelated. For example, it was envisaged that most of the issues which emerged from the discussions with teachers and the analysis of syllabuses would need to be explored further in the questionnaire. Additionally, it allowed more than one perspective to illuminate the curriculum issues that have been identified.

Sample, Data Collection and Analysis

Interviews with teachers

The sample consisted of sixteen teachers who were currently heads of physical education departments in secondary schools. Eight were male and eight female, and each of the sex groupings contained four teachers under and four teachers over 40 years of age. The decision to group in this way was influenced by the suggestion from the review of literature that there may be age and sex variables in teachers' planning. Although the sample of sixteen teachers may be considered to be relatively small, interviewing and the subsequent analysis was an expensive and time-consuming process, and for the purposes of this 'first stage' analysis, the sample was considered to be satisfactory. It was anticipated that the resulting data would provide pertinent information about individual planning procedures and also help identify issues which could be probed more deeply in the questionnaire.

An interview can take several forms and three main types were identified by

Kerlinger (1973) and Moser and Kalton (1979) and were considered for use in this part of the research. These were structured, unstructured and partly-structured interviews. In the structured interview, the sequence and wording of the questions are fixed beforehand and there can be no deviation from the prepared schedule. Answers are recorded in a standardized form and are usually subjected to some form of statistical analysis. In contrast to this, the unstructured interview is more flexible and open-ended. Usually there is no prepared schedule and a 'psycho-analytic' approach is used which allows the respondent to talk widely about the topic. This type of approach is usually recommended when knowledge in the area is vague and the researcher is in the initial stages of an investigation. Because of the different wording that may be used for the same question, or the different questions used, it is difficult to summarize and quantify the data from different interviews. Indeed, Galtung (1967) suggests that data obtained through these different questions makes the answers difficult to compare. Neither of these two methods appeared to be entirely suitable to this study and this led to the consideration of a partly-structured approach. This type of interview prepares a number of main topics or areas which are covered in a fairly systematic way. Questions are prepared beforehand, but the order of posing the questions is not rigid and this gives the interviewer more opportunity to link the discussions and allow the interview to flow. However, all the questions are presented at some stage during the interview. The respondent too, has considerable freedom to answer the questions and develop his ideas in an open-ended manner. In view of the nature of the present research problem, it was decided to use the partly-structured approach and focus on those main areas of planning which have been identified in the review of literature *viz:* planning of courses; aims and objectives; content; method and evaluation.

There are a number of advantages and disadvantages to interviewing which need to be considered. The first problem relates to the interviewer. Conducting a partly-structured interview requires a great deal of tact and understanding on his part, and he must be aware that he can introduce bias to the procedure. This can sometimes be done unconsciously in subtle ways such as tone of voice, comments and gestures. The interviewer partly determines the form of the interview, the order of the questions and the data that is recorded. In this way he influences the interview perhaps more than he realizes, and this can affect the reliability of the whole process.

In attempting to prevent this taking place, the questions posed need to be clear and unambiguous, specifically related to the research problem, and must seek to elicit information which the respondent should have. The responses that are given will tend to have a richness of language and spontaneity which is lacking in structured interviews. If questions are misinterpreted or not understood, it is possible to reword them. One of the biggest advantages of this technique is that it allows the interviewer to probe areas in depth and get a better and fuller understanding of the issues under consideration.

One problem associated with a partly-structured interview will be the recording of data. The use of a tape recorder produces a permanent record and frees the interviewer to concentrate on the interview. However, it is possible that some teachers may object to this method of recording. The extent to which a tape recorder will inhibit a respondent is not clear and there will certainly be some individual variations. The biggest advantage lies in the fact than an accurate transcript can be formulated afterwards and the recall is not subject to personal bias. In this instance, the advantages seem to outweigh the disadvantages and it was decided to use a tape recorder to record all the interviews.

Selecting appropriate questions is critical to the interview and it was necessary to pre-test any proposed questions to ensure that they were pertinent to the issue and free of ambiguity. This was done partly through discussions with teachers, advisers and lecturers, and partly through a pilot interview with a member of the physical education profession using the final selection of questions. A head of department was chosen for the interview who was an experienced teacher in a large mixed school with male and female colleagues in the department.

Examining physical education syllabuses

Documentary evidence of the planning done by physical education teachers can be obtained through reference to written syllabuses. Each of these represents a personal document which will be unique to a school and will not be subject to investigator bias because it will have been written beforehand. However, this is not to say that there is no bias, as some of the syllabuses may have been produced at the request of the Headteacher or the advisory staff. The fact that the syllabus had been requested by a specific person will colour the contents to some degree. The extent to which the syllabus will be a true and accurate reflection of what is actually happening in the school must also be considered. This is not to suggest that there will be false statements, but that there may be areas of work which are left out or not given sufficient emphasis.

In this study it was intended to collect a sample of syllabuses from secondary schools in England and Wales which reflect types of school (Comprehensive, Grammar, Secondary Modern) and sex of school (Boys, Girls, Mixed). It proved difficult, however, to obtain a representative sample through a postal request and alternative methods had to be considered, such as approaches to advisory staff in education authorities.

The syllabus was analyzed to develop an overall picture of the way in which teachers structured their written syllabus, as well as to examine their style of presentation. Two separate analyzes were undertaken as follows:

1 The first analysis was carried out by three independent judges – a teacher who was currently head of a large physical education department in a mixed school, a lecturer in physical education with experience in schools and colleges of education, and an adviser who had special responsibility for physical education in schools. At least one man and one woman were

selected. Each judge was asked to suggest a weighting given to aims and objectives, content, method and evaluation for each syllabus. (This was the methodology used by Taylor (1970) in analyzing three academic subjects in the curriculum. By using the same approach, it was possible to make some comparisons with Taylor's findings).

2 The second analysis examined the content, format and style of presentation of each syllabus. This was done by the author by means of an analysis sheet. This sheet was compiled by listing important areas that were identified during the interviews with the sixteen teachers, as well as from an inspection of the syllabuses. The frequency with which each area appears in the syllabus was then examined. There are however, a number of disadvantages to this type of frequency analysis. The identification of a number of clear cut categories may sometimes make it difficult to place certain aspects of the syllabuses into such clearly defined compartments. Thus a subjective element of choice by the recorder will inevitably be involved. Another disadvantage, related to the total scores in each category, was the possibility that some categories may receive a low score and there will be a tendency to infer that they are relatively unimportant, whereas for a particular school, they may be important. Finally, not only will some syllabuses be longer than others, but the quality of written statements also differed. Thus the recording gave only quantitative information. However, in spite of these limitations, the use of frequency distributions in important areas did reveal some valuable and interesting data in relation to planning.

The questionnaire

A questionnaire was constructed which was intended to widen the range and scope of the study and examine some of the issues which had been identified. The sample consisted of approximately 800 schools in ten authorities in England and Wales. All secondary schools with intakes at 11, 12 and 13 years were included in the sample. For sampling purposes, a two-way stratification was used according to:

1 Region: North, South-East, East, West, Midlands and Wales.
2 Type of school: Comprehensive, Grammar, Secondary Modern/High.

The advantage of a mailed questionnaire over personal interviewing is that any interviewer bias is partly avoided. Answers are confidential and anonymous, and this is done in an attempt to elicit frank and honest answers. Large numbers all respond to the same written questions, the answers to which are pre-coded for statistical and computer analysis. However, it does not cater for detailed probing and there will inevitably be differences in question interpretation. For example, the division between 'very important' and 'important' will vary with each respondent. One of the biggest disadvantages is the notoriously low percentage returns. In an effort to offset this, permission was obtained from the Chief Education Officer in each of the ten education authorities to approach the schools, and personal letters were written to the Headteacher and head of department explaining the reasons for the survey. A commitment was also given to make the findings available through in-service courses and publications. Care was taken with the presentation and format to ensure an immaculate presentation.

As in the interviewing technique, the framing of the questions is critical to the success of a survey, and in an effort to achieve this, three pilot surveys were conducted. The first preliminary check, in an attempt to validate the questionnaire, was carried out by asking three lecturer colleagues to complete the questionnaire, offer comments on any aspects which were not clear and then discuss the purpose of the survey. This resulted in some modifications, and the amended document was then scrutinized by three University staff who lectured in education. After this, the questionnaire was piloted in approximately 40 schools in different authorities from those to be used in the national sample. It was envisaged that some questions which reflect teachers' attitudes would need additional returns from approximately another 40 schools in order that a preliminary statistical analysis could be conducted. All the preliminary information was fed into a computer to ensure there were no errors in data presentation. These preliminary stages ensured that a reasonably reliable and valid questionnaire was presented to the sample. In addition, two follow-up requests were made to schools who did not reply.

The validated questionnaire was designed to allow the data to be processed by computer by means of the Statistical Package for the Social Sciences. After examining the distribution of each of the variables, this was followed by a more analytic approach which examined the relationships between the variables and between the variables and the sub-sections of the sample. In addition, factor analysis techniques were used to identify a small number of factors, or groups of items, which were used to identify criteria in teachers' planning. Thus, two main approaches were used:

1 *Descriptive.* Statistics were run on the questionnaire responses to give the counts, means, standard deviations, percentages and distribution of data.
2 *Analytical.* The main approaches used were:
   a) chi-square to investigate the relationship between variables,
   b) factor analysis to examine the underlying dimensions influencing teachers' planning.
   c) analysis of variance to examine the means of sub-sections of the sample (e.g. age and sex of teacher, size and type of school) in the areas of influencing factors, purposes of planning and methods of evaluation.

3 Interviewing Teachers: "What One Gains at College is the Last Real Guidance One Gets"

The literature has suggested that there is no single way in which teachers plan their courses. The manner in which programmes are planned and the order that is followed varies greatly. However, for a course to be effective it is essential that some preliminary planning is carried out and this is part of the professional responsibility of every teacher. The plan should include some indication of the aims and objectives to be achieved and give direction to the teaching and learning process. The coherence of the total course should be apparent together with the kinds of evaluation procedures to be used. In order to ascertain the manner in which teachers plan their physical education curriculum in secondary schools, it was decided that the first stage in this section of the enquiry should involve some contact with teachers in the schools. This was an attempt to start at the 'grass roots' level of curriculum planning which would help to shape future developments in the research.

Curriculum planning in physical education is a comparatively recent addition to the syllabus in colleges of education. There are therefore many teachers who have not received formal instruction in this important area. Even with in-service training, the developments have been spasmodic, unco-ordinated and diversified. Organizations such as the Nuffield Foundation and the Schools Council have both made major contributions to the development of curriculum planning in nearly all subjects on the school curriculum. It is regrettable that one subject that has not been the focus for such a study is physical education. The Schools Council Enquiry in Physical Education which was conducted in 1970–71, was merely the first step towards providing a basis for a curriculum development project at a later stage. Several projects have been submitted to national organizations since the preliminary enquiry, and it is a matter of some concern that the necessary funds have not yet been made available for further development.

It does appear that when physical education teachers plan their curriculum they have certain principles in mind, for, the content revolves round the six main activities of athletics, dance, games, gymnastics, swimming and outdoor activities. Some documentation is available concerning the aims behind the subject, the learning experiences and the teaching methods, but reliable and well validated techniques of evaluation are generally lacking. What is far from clear is the importance that teachers attach to each of these main areas of curriculum planning and the order in which they are used. It was hoped that discussion with teachers would help to give some answers to these two important variables.

Conducting discussions with individual teachers is a time consuming process. Nevertheless it was felt to be important that the initial enquiry into the planning of the physical education curriculum should be with the people who actually do the work. It was decided to approach sixteen heads of physical education departments, for this would enable comparisons to be made on the criteria of sex and age. The teachers agreed to take part in a taped discussion which would last for approximately one hour. Guarantees were given concerning the anonimity and confidentiality of the name of the school and the teacher.

The sixteen heads of physical education departments were selected on advice from the local advisory staff, based on two criteria:

1 Sex: eight men and eight women
2 Age: each of the sex groupings to contain four teachers over and four teachers under 40 years of age

All the teachers were from the same education authority and taught in a variety of schools, *viz:* comprehensive, grammar, independent and technical. The majority were known personally to the writer through in-service courses and teaching practice supervision of students. In all, eighteen teachers were approached, as two female teachers in the over 40 category were unable to take part. The size of the departments in these schools varied considerably, the smallest having one assistant teacher and the largest six.

Structuring the discussion

Before the interview started, it was stated that the discussion was to be open-ended and partly-structured. Some questions were asked which would give focus to the discussion, but it was important to realize that there were no right or wrong answers. The teachers were urged to say how they felt and what they did in relation to the planning of their courses. It was obvious that some teachers would be more forthcoming under these circumstances than others. Some required guiding whilst others needed prompting with specific questions.

The discussion was divided into six main areas. These were concerned with:

1 Planning of courses
2 Aims and objectives

3 Content
4 Learning experiences and teaching method
5 Evaluation
6 Reactions of teachers

These were the major components of the taped interview and approximately ten to fifteen minutes were allocated to each section. It was decided to follow this sequence in each case. This enabled a comparison to be made of each section according to the groupings identified in the sample.

It was felt advisable to have a bank of questions readily available in order to prompt those teachers who had difficulty in expressing themselves. Questions were prepared under each of the six sections, as well as a list of supplementary questions. It was important to ensure that pertinent questions were being asked and the final selection was only made after a number of consultations with experienced teachers, lecturers and advisers in the profession (See Appendix A). The questions were of two types. The first type asked for the teachers' opinions about key issues in the six main areas, a typical question here being, 'How do you judge the success of a course?' The second elicited more factual information about planning procedures. Wherever it was considered appropriate, the teachers were asked to amplify their answers. It was important that the interviewer should not stick rigidly to the list of questions. If the discussion was to have continuity and coherence, then questions and comments should arise logically from the preceding statements. Apart from trained personnel, most people do have some inhibitions when their opinions and views are being recorded. In an attempt to offset this, general encouragement was given through visual and verbal reinforcement.

The success of this interview technique depended a great deal upon the expertise of the interviewer. The teacher must be allowed to relax as much as possible under these circumstances. Accordingly, it was decided to conduct each interview at the school where the teacher would at least be in familiar surroundings. There were two exceptions to this when it was more convenient for the teacher to take part in the discussions outside the school. Prior to the interview, at least half-an-hour was spent in general conversation which helped to create a more relaxed situation. Each teacher was contacted personally by telephone and asked to participate in the project. A brief outline of the purpose of the discussion was given and stress laid on the importance of confidentiality and the fact that the ideas that were to be discussed would influence the future development of the research. The application of many research projects to the classroom situation is often questioned, but here was an opportunity for the teachers to be active participants, not only in the procedure of interviewing, but also in the development of curriculum planning. Subsequent to their acceptance, a letter was sent to each of the sixteen teachers thanking them for agreeing to participate and outlining in a little more detail the main areas to be discussed. This was sent at least one week prior to the meeting to allow the teachers some opportunity to present considered opinions.

A pilot interview based on the above ideas was considered essential in order to assess the suitability of the questions as well as to induct the author into this particular interviewing technique. An experienced male head of a physical education department was approached who readily agreed to participate. This enabled the interviewer to become more familiar with the process and to be more aware of any pitfalls. As a result of the pilot interview several points were noted which were helpful at later stages. These included:

1 a request for a less demanding start,
2 a brief outline of the research project at the beginning,
3 the sensitivity of teachers being questioned about their physical education curriculum,
4 the slight apprehension that teachers have about taking part in tape recorded discussions,
5 the importance of natural development and logical discussion,
6 an awareness not to interrupt silences too soon,
7 some reframing of questions to avoid ambiguity.

The alterations that were made regarding the subsequent interviews were purely on 'interviewing technique' and there was no revision regarding the content which was still to consist of the six main areas mentioned previously.

An analysis was made of the discussions that were conducted with the sixteen teachers and the various answers, where appropriate, were allocated to each section according to the two variables of sex and age. The results of this analysis are set out in the following pages.

Planning of Courses

Factors in planning

The analysis revealed many variables, but some common factors were apparent. These included the qualifications, interests and abilities of the qualified physical education staff and the academic staff. A great disparity was noted between the amount of help offered by the male and female academic staff. There was rarely any help forthcoming from female colleagues. In contrast, one male teacher made particular reference to the 'outstanding help from the male staff'. Staffing was often supplemented by outside qualified coaches who made a magnificent contribution to the range.

Facilities inevitably influence the types of activity that can be included in the programme and nearly all the teachers made reference to the facilities available in their schools. At some stage in the discussions ten teachers remarked on some inadequacies in their school provision. These ranged from a desire for another gymnasium to additional equipment with which to play certain games. Physical education equipment is very expensive and women teachers particularly were concerned about the low level of financial provision. Some of the schools were situated near to community sports centres and, with one exception, where too much travelling time was involved, all the schools made extensive use of these extra facilities. This partly alleviated the problem of inadequate resources in some schools.

The time allocated to physical education on the school timetable was a central factor in planning and was referred to by nearly all the teachers. The priority given to the planning of the physical education timetable varied from one comprehensive school where the teacher stated that the 'school timetable was built round us' to a girls' independent school where the physical education was planned after the academic timetable. Many timetable constraints such as short periods, the inability to block time, and academic subject preference all had an effect on overall planning.

The traditions of the school seemed to be an influencing factor for men as it was specifically mentioned on four occasions. It was not referred to once by the women teachers. This could not be accounted for by the age and type of school as some, where women teachers were in charge of the physical education, were long established schools and, in some cases, mixed schools. Perhaps it may also have reflected the greater emphasis that is placed on the playing of team games and traditions that have been established with other institutions. Sport in the local area was similarly mentioned only by the men teachers and may reflect their desire to offer an outlet for the sporting prowess of their children within the local community. This seemed to suggest that the men questioned probably gave greater emphasis to school traditions and local sport.

The actual activities offered were mentioned frequently and are analyzed in detail later in this chapter under Content. There was a general concern by the teachers to cater for all children and to give a good groundwork as well as to expose them to a fairly wide range of activities. This usually took the form of a 'common core' for the first three years followed by an increasing range of options. It was also clear that the actual content of the physical education curriculum figured prominently in the initial stages of planning.

Women teachers referred to children, their choices and individual differences, more frequently than their male counterparts in this section. However, it would be quite wrong to draw inferences from this fact as the needs and abilities of children were mentioned throughout the discussions by every teacher. This was perhaps highlighted by one young male teacher who stated that, 'children's needs can be taken as read – that's my existence here. Everything is built around and upon their needs and I aim to facilitate them'.

A factor mentioned by one male teacher was the importance of democratic decision-making. By this he meant the involvement of his colleagues in policy-making. Again, it must not be implied that departments in other schools were undemocratic, in fact, quite the reverse was revealed. It is just that one teacher regarded it to be of sufficient importance to give it a specific mention when considering his planning procedures.

Written syllabus

Each head of department stated that there was a written syllabus available in the school. The length of these varied from just a few pages to one that was approximately 200 pages. Some had been in existence for a number of years with apparently little change and had evolved into a fairly stable document. Others had been written quite recently for a variety of reasons. One newly appointed teacher made three visits to the school prior to his appointment in order that a syllabus would be available on his arrival. Whilst this proved to be moderately successful, he rewrote it at the end of the first year. Another teacher scrapped the original syllabus he had inherited for the simple reason that it was not being followed and was therefore not a true reflection of the work that was taking place. Three had written or revised their syllabuses quite recently because of visits from the local physical education advisory staff. For two young female teachers, this had been partly a collation and rationalization of statements already in existence. As one remarked, 'Up until then it had been on tatty bits of paper'. An older male teacher spoke highly of the advice and assistance that he had received from the local physical education adviser in revising his syllabus and stated that he 'found the exercise interesting'. Two young teachers were undergoing major reviews of their syllabuses. In one case this was the second within five years, whilst the other was still reviewing three years after her appointment as head of the department. One older woman teacher stated that 'We don't need to write a lot down'. (There were two staff in the department who had been colleagues for a long time). Of some concern is the quotation 'It is written down and some of it makes nonsense. I keep adding and cutting out'. Perhaps the wrong parts were being amended and this appeared to be a case for some expert advice.

Some syllabuses were formally reviewed by the whole department once a year and staff were encouraged to make comments and up-date those aspects which needed it. Quite often members of staff who had strengths in a particular area were given the responsibility of writing the syllabus for that area which was then incorporated into the department syllabus.

It is gratifying to record that there was a written syllabus in each of the sixteen schools. These ranged from those that were constantly under review with external advice to those that had become stable over the years. Some had been in existence for many years while others had been written or rewritten quite recently. Statements which indicated that the syllabus might not be an accurate reflection of the work in progress raised doubts about their validity.

Syllabus change

In all instances it was clear that any member of the department could initiate change. The method by which this was achieved varied considerably. The most common method was through formal department or faculty meetings where all members of the department had the opportunity to place items on the agenda for discussion. The change had to be approved by the departmental head and most of them welcomed constructive suggestions. One older teacher even referred to the 'first-rate' ideas that he had received from his assistant. These ranged from the introduction of new teaching strategies to the reformulation of sections of the syllabus. When individual members of staff have responsibility for constructing and writing parts of the syllabus they must feel that they are making a positive contribution and this should alleviate any feelings that the syllabus is being imposed from above. In less structured departments informal discussion took place at irregular intervals and one younger woman teacher stated that she 'hoped to remember the points when writing the syllabus and would hopefully incorporate them'.

Departmental guidelines

In response to the question 'Do colleagues have clear guidelines?' it became apparent that the majority of departmental heads gave very clear guidelines to their physical education colleagues through meetings and copies of the syllabus. One young male teacher stated that, 'the syllabus is examined at the beginning of every term. The director of each activity brings out points of emphasis for the term, coaching methods and new literature'. There was general agreement concerning what to teach and when to teach it but the suggestion that the teaching style could be imposed was rejected. Staff were expected to follow the syllabus and in some cases it was 'very much prescribed'. One young female teacher remarked, 'I don't mind the order they do it in provided the work is covered'.

A rather different picture emerged for the academic staff who taught physical education. Usually they helped with the coaching of games and the fact that they were practising games players and 'know more or less how to approach something' seemed to suffice in one instance. Another teacher expressed concern about the unsatisfactory nature of academic staff teaching physical education but suggested that there was 'no way round it'. Yet another gave verbal instructions each week on the arrival of the staff prior to teaching the lesson. Having made this analysis for this particular question, I would hasten to add that most teachers were very appreciative of the help and enthusiasm that academic staff made to physical education both in lesson time and after school.

Three teachers, all in the upper age bracket, were less specific in issuing guidelines. One remarked that the activity was decided, but 'what they do is largely left to them'. Another stated, 'I give them a broad outline. I tell them what activity to cover. In gymnastics I tell them to find out what the children have done and they then develop their work from that. I might suggest a few themes'. There was another instance where the subject area was specified but not what was taught in a lesson. This was highlighted by the statement, 'I wouldn't dream of telling her what to do'.

Although there were a few notable exceptions, the majority of departmental heads issued clear verbal and written guidelines to their physical education colleagues about the programme and the work to be covered. The guidelines to the academic staff appeared to be less specific and left something to be desired.

Departmental meetings

One female and four male teachers gave a positive reply to the question about departmental meetings. In most cases this consisted of a monthly meeting with an agenda but the discussion was generally of a semi-formal nature. Sometimes staff met in the lunch hour or after school on their own instigations, but in two instances the school organization required departments to meet on three occasions each term. However, these meetings were not time-tabled as part of the school day.

Two female teachers stated that they had one formal meeting with their department prior to the academic year. This was followed in one case by informal daily discussion without any more formally arranged meetings. The other attempted to call a meeting termly in order to 'look back and ahead' over the curriculum as well as assessing progress.

The importance of ensuring that everyone had an opportunity to contribute to curriculum planning was felt to be an essential part of democratic procedures and the open forum of departmental discussion played a vital role in this process. This point was remarked upon on more than one occasion.

The majority of teachers in the sample did not have full departmental meetings. Of the men teachers, one said that he would welcome a move towards this within the school organization, while another currently met with the head of girls' physical education, but could foresee the whole department meeting in the very near future. Another stated that he and his long-serving colleague, 'Get our heads together once a year. This is the programme that has served us well for 20 years'. Minor adjustments to the curriculum had been made and they had 'moved a little with the times'. Incidental and informal termly talks were referred to. Quite a unique setting was described by one teacher who, with his department, 'spent the evening in a pub and planned the syllabus in 3½ hours and any problems were sorted out in five minutes'. Similarly, at the start of term, he asked, 'Is everything OK?' If it was not alright, he called the staff in to resolve the problem. The women teachers also reported meetings of an informal kind. One remarked that with a small staff it was possible to 'see each other at lunch times and that's it'. In another school the girls' physical education staff was supposed to meet under the overall Head of Faculty but hadn't yet done so. One feature of teaching physical education is that staff mix with their colleagues in the department more frequently than in other subjects. This is partly because of the proximity of changing rooms and facilities which facilitates informal contact. This is perhaps exemplified by the remark 'We work so closely together. It is better to sit on the table at the end of a lesson and discuss informally'. Whilst recognizing that this has certain advantages relating to the everyday happenings at the time, the teacher hadn't really discussed the syllabus with her colleague.

What is abundantly clear is that there is no one method that is used by all departments. They are very varied and range from formal meetings with structured agendas to informal and spontaneous gatherings with unstructured discussion.

Boys' and girls' programmes

When planning the physical education curriculum in a mixed school, consideration needs to be given to the boys' and girls' programmes. Are they to be planned quite separately or integrated to some degree? This is a question that must be resolved at a very early stage. All the women teachers reported that the programmes were planned separately, although one said 'that it isn't because I wish it' but that it was a legacy from the past and that her ideas differed from those of her male colleague. The only co-ordination within the programme occurred over the organization of facilities.

With one exception the male teachers regarded the curriculum as a whole and not as two separate parts. 'A total physical education programme which is planned together' was given as one description. This does not infer that boys and girls always worked together – particularly in the first three years. However, the work of the boys and girls was seen as a joint enterprise and it was by common agreement that they should work in single sex classes. 'A mixed department under my guidance' and a 'joint department' were phrases used to describe this particular aspect of planning. The exception referred to the boys' and girls' sections being quite autonomous and the only integration related to the use of facilities.

Community facilities

Where suitable community facilities existed and they were within reasonable travelling distance, the schools tended to use them. One school in close proximity to a Sports Centre with a wide range of facilities used them on four occasions each week. It was interesting that some reciprocal arrangements were reported of the local community using the school facilities. The opportunity to use additional facilities enabled a wider range of activities to be offered such as squash, swimming and ski-ing. This provided an extension to the normal physical education curriculum but all teachers stressed how important it was that the children were always under instruction. There is no doubt that community provision of this nature can and does influence the school curriculum. This fact is highlighted by the teacher who said, 'The only radical change in the syllabus occurred when we were able to use the local Sports

Centre facilities'. One teacher expressed some doubts about too many options being offered but this would seem to be a matter of sensible planning rather than an argument against their use.

Guidelines for planning

Every teacher was asked if guidelines would be helpful when planning their physical education syllabus. The analysis of their replies is made through extracts of statements and summaries in each of the four catgories.

Men teachers over 40 years:
"I would appreciate something written down".
"What one gains at college is the last real guidance we get".
"My physical education programme is influenced by this. It could be helpful to the profession – probably for the younger teacher who would like something to grasp at when he is not sure where he is going and how he is going to get there".

Men teachers under 40 years reported:
"I think it would be helpful but the situation would be different for each teacher".
"I think they would. I gave the Headmaster a copy of the syllabus, but I have never seen another physical education syllabus".
"I think it certainly would be of use – particularly for in-service courses".

Women teachers over 40 years:
"The Headmistress has a copy of the time-table, but not the content syllabus".
"Yes, I would indeed. I am fortunate to have a lot of help from my two colleagues".
"I didn't find the syllabus easy to write and would appreciate guidelines".
"I only once got advice from a local in-service course. It is a mistake not to have seen other syllabuses".

Women teachers under 40 years reported:
"When I did mine I had no idea whether I had done the right thing. I found it difficult to write because I have never worked under a head of department before".
"No-one has ever read my syllabus or questioned me about the programme".
"Oh yes, definitely. It is really lacking. This was a problem".

> "This is the only syllabus I have ever seen. The Headmaster probably hasn't seen it".
> "It is very difficult to think of the main factors – almost impossible in fact".

It was clear that all the teachers felt that some framework or guidelines to planning the physical education curriculum would be helpful to the profession. Clearly it would be impossible to lay down a rigid format because of the uniqueness of every school. However, a basic outline with freedom to interpret seemed to be something that would be welcomed. The actual syllabuses appeared to have a rather restricted circulation outside their own departments. It was quite surprising that a large number of teachers had never seen another physical education syllabus or even the syllabus of another subject in their own school.

Aims and objectives

Aims

As there are conflicting definitions in the literature between aims and objectives, it is important to make a clear distinction at the outset. Aims are related to the long-term goals of physical education and are generally directional in nature, whereas objectives are more short-term and can be specified in relation to lessons or schemes of work. In posing the question 'What are the main aims you hope physical education achieves in your school?', we are concerned with the aims of the subject.

The sixteen teachers made twenty-three separate claims for the effect of physical education in this section and they are set out in diagrammatic form in *Table 1* according to the sex and age variables. The first comment on the results is a critical one. Although a distinction had been made earlier between aims and objectives, it appeared that a few teachers did not appreciate the difference, as some of the so-called aims in *Table 1* might be labelled objectives. For example, 'success in a particular activity' might be regarded as relatively short-term in duration. With this reservation, the aims in the first column are listed in the terminology used by the teachers and where there appeared to be areas of overlap, these have been recorded against a common heading. A number of comparisons can be made. *Table 2* shows the number of recordings and the number of aims made by the teachers according to the sex and age variables.

The number of claims made by both groups of men and the older women teachers are reasonably consistent in relation to recordings and aims. However, it is important to note that this does not imply that each group recorded similar scores against the same aim. The group which showed a marked

Table 1. Aims of physical education: teachers' recordings according to sex and age variables.

Aims	Men 40+				Men 40−				Women 40+				Women 40−				Total
Skill acquisition	x	x		x		x	x	x	x	x			x	x	x	x	12
Recreation for Leisure	x	x	x	x	x		x	x	x		x	x	x	x			12
Health and Fitness	x	x		x	x	x	x	x				x			x	x	10
Socialization						x		x			x	x	x	x	x	x	8
Enjoyment	x			x		x			x	x	x	x		x			8
Fair Play			x					x			x						3
Sportsmanship						x							x			x	3
Success				x	x			x									3
Activity				x	x									x			3
Knowledge									x		x			x			3
Body Awareness											x		x			x	3
Character Building										x	x						2
Realize Potential													x		x		2
Doing One's Best			x														1
Broad Range of Activity								x									1
Passing 'O' Levels										x							1
Challenge													x				1
Competition													x				1
Leadership																x	1
Self-Discipline															x		1
Self Confidence															x		1
Expression													x				1
Aesthetic Appreciation																x	1

Table 2. Aims of physical education: number of recordings according to sex and age variables.

	Number of Recordings	Number of aims
Men 40+	16	8
Men 40−	19	10
Women 40+	19	10
Women 40−	28	17

difference was the younger women teachers who made many more recordings against a greater number of aims.

In a comparison between the sexes, men teachers made thirty-five recordings against eleven different aims. This contrasted markedly with the forty-seven recordings against twenty aims by the women teachers. There was no doubt that women teachers in the sample made many more claims than their male colleagues in a wider range of aims.

The aims given greatest importance by the total sample were skill acquisition (12), recreation for leisure (12), health and fitness (10), socialization (8) and enjoyment (8). (The number in brackets denotes the number of teachers who referred to that particular aim). As is to be expected, the acquisition of motor skills is one of the prime aims of physical education and this was the aim most frequently referred to. Perhaps the surprising fact is that it was not stated by all the teachers, but two men and two women did not mention this during the discussions. At the other extreme, one teacher specifically stated that his entire curriculum was 'now mainly skill acquisition'

Of similar importance was recreation for leisure which was mentioned by seven men and five women. There was certainly concern that the children should continue to participate in physical activity once they left school and some staff had established sound links with local clubs and sports centres. One young teacher even intended to circulate a questionnaire to some of his former pupils in order to discover their levels of participation. The desire to develop a lasting interest in the subject throughout life was certainly a recurring theme.

The development of health and fitness was specified by seven of the eight male teachers. The one exception stated, 'Health education was not covered', but he was rather self-critical of this fact. Some of the schools used very objective means for determining fitness levels either through national norm tables or local adaptations of these. This kind of testing gave rise to the statement '... included now because we found the boys weak in the upper body'. Certainly health, hygiene and personal standards in this area were seen as important aims of the physical education curriculum. This aspect did not assume quite the same status for women teachers as it was not only mentioned by a fewer number, but also interpreted slightly differently. Jogging and the Health Council were mentioned in this context, as well as posture, keep fit and diet. Even when it was regarded as an aim, it was certainly put in its place by one teacher when she said, 'We under-rate and under-play it. It is a part, but not as important as the others mentioned'.

Eight teachers altogether, six of whom were women, with six of the total in the younger age category, mentioned the social benefits of the subject which included adjusting to others, group relationships, team work, co-operation and working together for a common goal.

The importance of enjoyment by the children through the physical activity offered in the curriculum was stated on eight occasions, of which six were in the older age bracket. In response to this question, one teacher's first words were, 'First of all, enjoyment'. Another stated, 'Encourage a sense of enjoyment' and repeated it in an attempt to emphasize the point. 'Maximum activity with enjoyment' and 'Enjoyment comes out of what we do' are other relevant quotations. Whilst it would be difficult to substantiate the inclusion of a subject in the school curriculum purely on the grounds of enjoyment, there was no doubt that this aspect was rated highly by many teachers and was regarded as an essential ingredient to physical education.

The five aims discussed above were referred to on eight or more occasions by the teachers in the sample. The next six aims in the rank order were each referred to on three occasions. These included fair play in respect of the laws and other people (which may be partly linked with moral education) and sportsmanship which related to children getting to know the meaning of 'good sport', winning and losing. The aim of sportsmanship was only mentioned by younger teachers. It is possible to argue that these two aims should be linked together under a broader category, but as the sample is small and the purpose of the analysis is to depict what the teachers felt was important in their schools, the two aims are left separate. Success appeared to be a specific aim for men teachers as it was only mentioned by them and was highlighted by one teacher who said, 'It is vitally important to me that I give every boy who comes to my subject something that he can do'. Although success was not mentioned by thirteen teachers, it could be argued that they considered it to be implicit in their work and did not feel the need to specify success as a separate aim. Another aim was activity. Presumably this is an integral part of physical education and it is impossible to participate in the subject without this kind of involvement. The fear that there is a trend away from the physical came out from the statement, 'We get many high flown aims from books, but physical education is mainly activity'. Three women teachers regarded a knowledge of body movement, rules and tactics in games and the ability to spectate intelligently as important. A similar number of women teachers considered body awareness to be an aim. One teacher even stated that physical education was concerned with 'a complete awareness of the body' and that everything else was subsidiary to this.

Regarding the remaining aims, the claim that physical education can play a part in character building was mentioned twice by older women teachers. One stated that, 'The discipline that comes from games would help them as young adults to discipline their own lives which is sadly lacking'. Two young teachers considered that the subject offered children the opportunity to realize their potential in a variety of ways and that this was especially true for remedial children who had perhaps experienced little success in the academic sphere of school life.

A number of additional aims were mentioned once. One older male teacher was concerned that children have the satisfaction of 'Doing their best' within their own limits, while a younger male teacher considered the offering of a broad base of activity essential in order that children could make an informed choice at the end and that this would also 'extend the pinnacle of expertise'. The claim that 'Physical education enhances the chances of passing O-levels' is not one that has been substantiated, but one older woman teacher felt it was worthy of mention. The remaining aims were all stated by younger female teachers and were concerned with children accepting challenges, coping with competition and experiencing leadership. The self-discipline and self-confidence that can develop through participation in physical education was also noted. Finally, an opportunity to learn about expression in gymnastics and dance, and the ability to make an aesthetic appreciation and recognize skilled movement through their own experience were considered to be important.

Additional points that were revealed suggested that there may be 'written aims' at the front of a syllabus but that these may not necessarily reflect the direction or emphasis of the department in the school. This is surely a matter for concern and may partly explain the reason for aims not being realized, and the gap that exists between theory and practice. The statement that, 'We owe something to society to develop children' seems the least that teachers can do considering that society is responsible for establishing and financing educational institutions for this very purpose.

Communicating aims and objectives

Most teachers did not communicate their aims to the children. It was certainly never done formally or written down for the pupils to see. In one school, the values of physical education were debated on an *ad hoc* basis in English lessons, but this was not formally planned. It was also suggested that the aims percolated to the children through the extra-curricular clubs. One teacher said, 'Not specifically, but broadly "Yes" when the opportunity arrives'. This was because he felt that there was a need to give children the reasons for studying the subject. The incidental nature of justifying the subject to children was stated in another discussion and generally this was attempted with the more senior pupils. Some teachers did not discuss their aims at all and this was substantiated by the quotations, 'We have never asked them and they have never asked us', and 'We don't intellectualize with the children'. Another stated, 'No, we don't have time. I wonder if boys are capable of realizing what we are trying to achieve'. It seems, therefore, that if aims are not clearly enunciated, the children will pick up the purposes of the subject in an incidental way and that these will vary according to the individual and the nature of his experiences.

The picture changed slightly with shorter-term objectives where there was some suggestion that verbal objectives were stated at the beginning of a block of work. 'Objectives give direction' said one teacher, but no-one suggested that it was done systematically throughout the department. In one school it was more likely to occur with the CSE group studying physical education with a Mode III syllabus that was internally formulated and externally moderated. This may be attributed to the fact that the Examination Board required a written syllabus with the objectives clearly stated. Another similar example occurred in a school with a very elaborate syllabus where the teachers gave the children a general outline of the term's work. The inference here is that the more detailed the planning, the more likely it is that techers will be able to give their pupils a clear indication of the work upon which they are about to embark.

In summary, the most common aims were skill acquisition, recreation for leisure, health and fitness, socialization and enjoyment, but some differences were revealed between male and female, and older and younger teachers (under 40 years). In addition, a large number of other claims were made, each one being supported by only a few teachers. From the transcripts of the interviews, it was apparent that the distinction between aims and objectives was not clear to all the teachers. It is possible to argue that one cannot prescribe aims and objectives for all aspects of physical education, but none of the teachers raised this particular point. In terms of communication, there was a greater likelihood that teachers would communicate the short-term objectives to children rather than the longer-term aims. The incidental and infrequent manner of communicating the aims of physical education to children gives cause for concern. Perhaps a more definite and clearly defined strategy should be adopted.

Content

Common core

All the secondary schools in the sample had a compulsory common core of activities. Usually this took place in the first three years and consisted of a selection from the major winter/summer games, gymnastics, swimming, athletics and dance. However, the amount of time allocated varied considerably because of the number and length of the timetabled lessons. Not every activity was offered in each year, although most were. The usual exception was swimming where time, expense and community facilities limited it to the first year. One girls' school did not include dance because the teacher was 'not keen' and considered other activities to have priority. Most schools were allocated three or four periods a week on the timetable in order to complete this core of work although one independent school used five or six periods.

Occasionally there was a slight broadening of the activities being offered in the third year. There was agreement between all four categories in the sample that the first three years should provide a broad based experience from which informed choice could be made at a later stage. All the classes came to physical education in their normal units and were therefore in mixed ability groups. One young female teacher was concerned about this because she stated, 'The standard of the children is poor and could be raised. There is a place for removing the very good and the bad. The very good become frustrated and lose interest'. She obviously had reservations about teaching mixed ability groups and strongly favoured streaming.

Optional activities

All the schools offered some choice within the physical education curriculum in the fourth and fifth years. The majority had chosen to offer some compulsory and some optional activities, but one school had chosen a totally optional programme for their pupils in the fifth year. They had even gone so far as to change the name to recreational education and were satisfied that the courses were a success. One young woman teacher had tried a completely optional programme and had returned to a restricted range because she said, 'Too much choice was ruining standards'. The statement that, 'If children can choose, it will keep their interest' is not necessarily true, but it can certainly help if they know that their choices are being taken into consideration. One school circulated a questionnaire to the girls at the end of the fifth year and planned the sixth form work accordingly. Another older woman teacher adopted a similar approach and allowed the democratic choice of the children to determine the activity emphasis. When the work of the sixth forms was examined, an even wider range of options was in operation. It was clear that the longer the pupils remained in school, the wider was the choice that was offered.

Children were required to remain with their choice for at least half-a-term and in some cases a full term. This was insisted upon by all but one of the teachers. The exception was a young woman teacher who allowed choice on a week to week basis. If standards are to improve and logical progression is to be developed, there is much to be said for the longer period of involvement. Again, there was one exception to the notion that there were actual teaching options. 'They should always be in a learning situation otherwise it is a waste of an afternoon' said one teacher, while another referred to them as 'teaching options and not recreational options'. The young male teacher who took a different view said, 'Options are recreational and not really under instruction'. It is important to say that the quality of the teaching depends to a large extent upon the quality and ability of the teacher. Many schools hired qualified professional coaches in a variety of activities such as badminton, fencing, archery and judo, in an attempt to increase the range and ensure adequate standards of teaching in a number of activities.

When the opportunity presented itself, two teachers used the optional activities programme to stream some groups according to ability. One reported that the groups were streamed in relation to their ability in games and hoped that it would improve the playing standard of the school teams.

Whether or not children should be allowed to opt out of physical education completely is a debatable issue. A wide spectrum of opinion revealed itself in the present sample. This ranged from the teacher who stated 'Physical education is compulsory throughout the school', to those who felt that the pupils themselves could make their own choice once they were in the sixth form. Where this choice did operate, a high proportion did opt out and this was mainly because of the pressures of academic work. In most cases a 'guided choice' operated. Some schools required those pupils who have ability to play team games and, if chosen, to represent the school. Others were guided to choose something but could opt out altogether either with the approval of the staff or of their own volition. A number of schools blocked the senior school physical education programme into one afternoon and linked it to voluntary or community service. This offered pupils an alternative to the normal programme.

Time allocation

The teachers were asked if they had ever done a 'time analysis' on their curriculum. This is a straightforward analysis which calculates the number of hours devoted to each activity termly, annually and over the whole curriculum. Aspects of work which are considered to be of greater importance are presumably allocated a substantial proportion of time. It should also ensure that there is a reasonable balance between different types of activities as well as showing how much time is devoted to aspects of the common core and the option programme. Of the sixteen teachers only one young male teacher had actually conducted the analysis to any depth. He had done this quite recently and had acted upon the findings. The results had shown that it was virtually impossible to achieve any depth in the option programme because of the time allocated and he had subsequently reduced the number of options offered in order to alleviate this problem. In this instance, the analysis had prompted a reappraisal of the curriculum which had led to some changes taking place.

Without having actually carried out the analysis, some of the teachers did comment on the allocation of time within their curriculum. Two teachers were 'horrified and staggered' how much time was spent in travelling, changing and showering for physical education. As a result, one teacher had decided to work in double periods to reduce changing time. There was an emphasis towards games, particularly in the autumn and spring terms, but the teachers who remarked on this were happy that this should be so. One said, 'There is a tremendous swing away from gymnastics in boys' schools. Not many like gymnastics these days. To go with the trend or answer the demand, we have moved away from gymnastics'. Some said they had considered 'balance' when preparing their syllabuses and that it was important the children experienced a variety of activities.

Award schemes

Many activities have a system of graded awards for children which sets standards for them to obtain. In terms of assessment, some are purely objective such as running or swimming distances in a specific time and others clearly state the criteria for satisfactory performance in activities such as gymnastics. Nearly all schools award certificates and/or badges which have great significance for the children. They are worn on track suits and clothing, and there is no doubt that they are a great motivating force in providing specific goals to aim for in skilled performance. Because of the individual nature of the motivation and the clear and objective assessment, it is possible to organize lessons of physical activity based solely on this format.

The question posed to the teachers asked if they used the award schemes in their physical education curriculum either in timetabled lessons or club activities. The replies were interesting and showed some clear divisions of opinion. Very few of the women teachers incorporated any of the award schemes into their lessons. In two schools where they did use them, they were of a very minor nature. Generally, they were not used and the following comments were not untypical:

> "Not in class time because there is enough to do".
> "I can't teach and do awards at the same time".
> "I felt guilty that I wasn't teaching when I used awards".

There appeared to be no objection to their use in extra-curricular activities and a limited range of award schemes were used. The BAGA (Gymnastic) awards were not used in two schools because they were related to Olympic gymnastics and were 'very narrow and restrictive'.

Men teachers in the over 40 category all used award schemes during lessons and in their club activities. The range of activities was greater than those mentioned by women teachers and in one school parents who had a coaching qualification in a particular sport helped in the club activities. Another school had developed its own standards which allowed every boy to be able to score points towards an elaborate system of House competition. The male teachers in the younger age range each presented a different viewpoint. One used them mainly in extra-curricular activities and would not use them in lessons because he felt that too much time was spent in assessment and not enough on teaching. Another allowed the children to practice for the awards during lessons but never tested during these periods. The same sentiment was expressed when he said, 'I can spend a lot of time testing and not enough teaching'. The third quite clearly expressed his attitude when he stated

'Award schemes are not used anywhere'. The last teacher had a contrary opinion to this, particularly concerning the 5 Star Awards in athletics when he remarked, 'I spend a fantastic number of hours on them. I think it is worth doing – just in lesson time'. He also utilized the soccer, gymnastic, swimming and trampoline schemes.

A complete spectrum of opinion was revealed regarding the use of award schemes in physical education. Women teachers did not use them to any great extent and certainly rarely in the normal time-table. Men teachers used more award schemes and used them more frequently. They were often utilized in lessons, but some younger teachers expressed concern that the assessment procedures were too time consuming and insisted that they were carried out during the club activities.

In summary, all the teachers indicated that they had a compulsory common core during the first three years from 11 to 14 years of age. This provided a broad base from which informed choice could be made in the upper school during the optional activities programme. Whether or not pupils should be allowed to opt out of physical education from the fifth form onwards is a contentious issue and a division of opinion was revealed. In many schools, a compromise was reached through counselling procedures and this seemed a sensible solution. Only one teacher had conducted an analysis of the time devoted to the various aspects of the physical education curriculum. The remainder had developed some intuitive feeling for balance within and between the different aspects of the subject. This was a pity because the data from the analysis can give rise to a number of pertinent questions concerning the emphasis and balance within the programme which might not otherwise be asked. The use of the national award schemes within the timetabled lesson was hotly debated and provoked a number of widely contrasting viewpoints. Provided the award schemes are used to supplement the programme and do not dictate what is taught, then they have much to offer. The extent to which they are used can then be left to the individual teacher.

Learning experiences and teaching method

Range of experiences

In putting the question, 'Do you try to ensure children experience a range of activities?', I wished to discover if the teachers consciously planned that the children should be exposed to a range of experiences, such as individual, team, expressive and mixed activities (where appropriate), in the physical education curriculum. Women teachers were not very forthcoming, except that the majority felt that this was done intuitively rather than something that was consciously planned. 'It so happens' and 'Nothing designed about it' were typical comments. Most felt that their programme did cover a range and some felt that guidelines would be helpful.

The majority of male teachers similarly considered their planning of a range of experiences to be mainly retrospective. One teacher said 'It is not necessarily planned that way but there is opportunity for this if they wish' and this reflected several of the discussions. The one notable exception was one young teacher who remarked, 'This was the way in which the syllabus was initiated. In Year 4, every child has had a wide range of individual, mixed, team and creative experiences'. He also commented that one of the disadvantages of specializing too early was that it restricted the broad range of experience that was necessary for an understanding of the subject. A number of schools felt that their programme did not cater for the expressive activities and others felt that the complete range was available for children to choose through the optional activities and extra-curricular work. The opportunity for boys and girls to work together was regarded as a 'tremendous social experience' by one teacher and many of the optional programmes specifically catered for this in their planning. The importance of competition was mentioned by two teachers, one of whom specifically referred to competitive form games in the first and second year. This approach created some problems. One was that the 'spares and left-overs' played with other pupils of comparable ability and the other was that the inter-house rivalry generated in the school was 'too much like war' and there were plans to make it less competitive.

Extra-curricular activities

Every head of department considered the extra-curricular work to be an essential aspect of their work. In response to how important extra-curricular activities were rated one teacher replied, 'Very, very, very highly. Very highly. It is the first question I put to intending staff. We just can't put in enough hours'. Lunch hours, after school, week-ends and holidays were times when clubs and teams assembled. Most regarded it as an extension of their normal work and believed it to be an implicit part of the job. It provided an opportunity to develop skill at all levels. The competitive nature of team games was stressed and at the same time the prestige attached to school fixtures was mentioned. This assumed varying degrees of importance from satisfactory levels of team success to achieving representation in area teams. The latter point was highlighted by the young male teacher who said, '9.0am. to 3.30.pm. is bread and butter, outside this is the cream on the cake. The higher aspects of physical education are achieved here. I am looking for high standards'. He went on to claim that, '. . . the only way that I can compete with academic subjects is through county representative players rather than the good programme I have in the school'. In this instance, the justification of the total physical education curriculum seemed to depend on the athletic prowess of a few children.

The men teachers were particularly appreciative of the help that was forthcoming from their colleagues and recognized the important part they played in the development of this aspect of school life. No such comments were made by the women teachers and in fact some specifically remarked on the fact that they received no assistance from the academic staff. Within their own departments, physical education teachers gave freely of their time, were nearly always available, and in one instance 'kept the House system alive'. In one boarding school another claim was made for the value of extra-curricular work where the teacher said that the children were lonely and desperately wanted attention. Occasionally, mention was made of the shortage of time during lunch hours and the fact that some children could not stay on after school. This obviously restricted the involvement of these children and may partly explain why some of the more able were steered towards clubs in the local area.

It was interesting to find out if all the clubs were open to all the children regardless of ability. All the women teachers stated that, in the first instance, this was the case but occasionally an age limit might be imposed. Team practices which started as open were sometimes reduced through poor attendance or inadequate skill levels. However, the majority of women were content to allow any child to attend any club. Even for team practices, strategies were adopted which allowed substitutions to take place and keep everyone involved. A similar situation was found for five of the men teachers. Comments such as 'interest is the only criteria – even for first team practices' and 'no-one should be excluded' tended to support this. Perhaps the clearest statement came from the young teacher who said, 'I welcome all children. It helps to improve standards. The poorer performer is just as important as the good performer. This might affect my team standards (I hope not) but it is a price I am prepared to pay'. The three exceptions had adopted a squad system for their teams, entry to which was by invitation and ability, and a truly open entry to other clubs such as gymnastics and archery. The pressures of, and the importance attached to, competitive sport would appear to be an influencing factor.

The overall impression gained from the discussions was one of considerable commitment by the physical education teaching staff to extra-curricular activities. This was further enhanced by many male colleagues who made substantial contributions in this area. The number of clubs in any one school varied according to the resources and facilities available, but it was pleasing to note that in one very large school with excellent facilities, the teacher reported, 'fifty to sixty clubs going all the time'.

Progressive planning

If there is to be progression in the curriculum this should not be a haphazard affair but something that is planned and worked for systematically. The teachers were asked if they had planned for progression during the academic year (horizontal) and between the years (vertical).

The majority of teachers stated that they did try to ensure that there was horizontal planning throughout a particular year. In some cases this was achieved through staff continuity and in others it was specifically built into the syllabus. The progression varied from precise specification to statements of faith, such as 'Yes – hopefully', and 'They are better, but I don't think I took this into consideration in building the syllabus'. One older male teacher regarded the progression as a 'weeding out for the squad system' and had a loose framework of progression that wasn't written down. The discussions with the younger women teachers were interesting. One was quite precise in the developments she hoped to obtain through the written syllabus and reviewed with her department at the end of every term to ensure that they were being achieved. Another had linked together themes in gymnastics and dance which was an attempt to achieve greater continuity and understanding. A third said there should be, but 'in practice, the children don't remember'. A young male teacher had devized teaching schedules for the first three years but was concerned about the great individual variations within classes. Because of the club coaching that was taking place in the locality, particularly in soccer, levels of aspiration and expectancy of the more able pupils were possibly not being met.

The importance given to the progression of learning experiences between the years is best exemplified by extracting a few statements from the discussions.

> "Oh yes, very much – especially in the development of games skills".
> "I can't really see how you can do it any other way".
> "It is intended, whether we achieve this I'm not sure".
> "Yes, staff take the same class for the first three years".
> "Year II builds on Year I etc. Set down in syllabus".
> "There is a record book in which staff record their work".
> "Yes, we aim to do this. Whether we succeed is another question".

The general impression of logical planning was not apparent in one school which had a syllabus for an activity which was not linked to any particular year. Teachers were free to extract from it and make their own decisions about the kind of learning experiences they offered the children. The head of department said, 'I don't plan to that extent, *e.g.* in basketball I do the following. . . . I can't vouch for the others in the department although I think they follow the same lines. I don't put it down on paper beforehand'.

The progressions that were noted were often tied to the more objective aspects of physical education in activities such as games and swimming where it was easier to be more precise in stating progressive stages, whereas gymnastics was only mentioned on one occasion. Not one referred to progression in the optional activities programme. All spoke about the work from the first to the third or fourth year and it may be that this part of the syllabus does have a coherence and structure which is lacking in some of the later work.

Some heads of departments checked with their colleagues that the work was being covered adequately, but this was the exception rather than the rule. One teacher ensured that her colleagues from other subject areas who helped with physical education were told what to teach and how to teach it and this again helped towards continuity within the vertical planning of the curriculum.

Inter-disciplinary studies

The question in this section asked if the physical education department was involved with any other department in the school in studying a topic through their different disciplines. Most responses showed that there was very little collaborative work of this nature taking place although there were isolated examples of links with science and drama. The scientific links were related to physiology, hygiene and measurement which was in turn linked to health and fitness. Two girls' departments were involved in dance drama and one young teacher expressed regret that there were no longer links with the creative arts, especially as dance used to be part of this faculty.

Two young men teachers expressed regret that there was not more co-operation with other departments. One made a general criticism of physical education departments for isolating themselves from the rest of the school curriculum. In his own school, he had made limited links with history and science, and some Newsom type activities, *eg.* photography and sport. The other teacher had tried a six week block of theory with fifth form pupils which was linked to a CSE Humanities project, but this had not been a success and said 'the children would sooner be active'.

There does seem to be some desire to be involved in interdisciplinary enquiry with other departments. However, the pressure of examinations in academic subjects made any immediate prospect of this being achieved rather remote.

Teaching styles

Because of the variety and diverse nature of many activities in physical education, the teachers were asked if they used different teaching styles during their working day. The older group of men teachers indicated that they tended to use the same style which was usually of a direct nature. Comments such as, 'I am fairly direct but still like to involve the children and their responses', 'mainly direct with some enquiry approach', and 'probably the same style because I have managed for a long time and we are fairly set in our ways' supported this suggestion. One head of department thought that his colleagues were more indirect in their approach but he stressed quite strongly that he made no attempt to impose any particular teaching method on them. There appeared to be very little conscious attempt by this group to vary the teaching style in relation to the activity.

A different profile was revealed by the women and younger men teachers. The latter group clearly showed that the needs and abilities of the children were a strong influencing factor. This was substantiated by a number of quotations, for example, 'I use a different style for different needs. It depends on the group of children' and 'Mine varies to some extent. It often varies because of the response of the pupils and their ability'. The overriding influence by the group of children on the teaching method to be adopted was quite clear. The actual content was subsidiary and this was confirmed by one teacher who said, 'The activity may possibly change my style but the children have the most infuence'.

Women teachers also used a variety of teaching styles and did not stick rigidly to one. The age and maturity of the children was mentioned and a more formal approach was adopted with the younger age groups. One young teacher also felt that a direct style was more suitable for 'less able' classes and that she had more freedom to experiment with 'brighter' classes. The activity did appear to be an influencing factor and in fact one older teacher remarked that she felt the 'activity dictated the style'. Educational gymnastics and dance were given as examples where problem-solving and guided discovery approaches were most suitable, whereas games was more direct. 'I can never see much variation in the teaching of games, mostly direct, mostly organization' was a quotation from the older group.

Differences are revealed by this analysis, whereby older men teachers tend to use a more directed approach to their teaching. Age and sex also appeared to be a variable in whether the nature of the activity or the needs of the children were of primary importance in influencing teaching styles.

Evaluation

Judging the success of courses

In many subjects on the school curriculum effectiveness is judged through the examination system, but this is not usually the case in physical education. When the teachers were asked how they judged the success of their courses in physical education, no clear pattern emerged between the four groups, but two older men teachers indicated they did not make a conscious attempt to evaluate. For one, the justification lay in the fact that 'the lads continue to play' and the school had an excellent tradition in competitive games, the other pointed out the difficulties in a large school and was 'happy to come through the day, let alone evaluate'.

The other teachers referred to the enjoyment the children got from the lessons as well as the general attitude, working atmosphere and demeanour that was generated throughout the school. Standards of work were mentioned on several occasions and these could be linked with skill learning and achieving competent levels of skilled performance. Some objectivity was mentioned in relation to evaluation of games playing ability. Inevitably the success and failure record of competitive teams was stated and the importance attached to it varied considerably. In one institution the 'school reputation was paramount', whilst another had a different perspective in which the excellence of a few was important, but of far greater significance was the fostering of good attitudes and the success of the teaching programme. A quotation which supported this said that the teacher 'wouldn't go to the cup cupboard – that is immaterial. I like to see the weakest lads are all competent and getting a reasonable amount of enjoyment'. The success and proficiency of gymnastic and dance display teams were also regarded as a shop window for the physical education department. Participation in post school recreation was included in two of the discussions.

Some objectivity was mentioned in measuring fitness levels. Two schools used fitness tests that were administered at least once a year and each child could assess his own progress. In schools where fifth and sixth form pupils could choose to opt out of physical education, this gave an objective measure of their keenness to carry on with the subject. However, it is true to say that some children were unable to continue because of time-table and academic constraints. In a school which had a large percentage of children opting out, the teacher felt this very keenly and said, 'I would say I'm not successful because I feel a failure when year five girls opt out'. The number of children who participated in clubs and teams out of school hours was another method teachers used to judge their success.

It is clear that teachers use a variety of criteria to judge the success of their physical education programmes and that each teacher uses a slightly different combination. Some objectivity is used to assist in making value judgements but it is doubtful if the evaluation is done in any systematic and methodical way. Some concern was also expressed about the time consuming nature of evaluation and it is essential that any testing procedures used must be easy and quick to administer.

Evaluating original aims

If there are agreed aims for a subject then it seemed reasonable to ask if the teachers tried to evaluate the work they do in respect of these aims at any stage during the course. Most replied that they did, although there were a number of serious reservations expressed about the way this was done and the extent of their effectiveness. The comment, 'It worries me that I haven't achieved what I set out to do' was not untypical. Occasionally it was discussed by the department but it was more likely to be informal. One teacher said, 'We talk about it . . . no real attempt is made to evaluate the success of our own teaching, except we are unconsciously aware that things are O.K.'. Another stated, 'Informally we agree that we do achieve them'.

One young teacher carried out this kind of evaluation 'usually when something goes wrong'. Occasionally she felt guilty about being complacent and suggested that she didn't consider this as deeply and as often as she should. When children lost interest it prompted her to think and ask, 'Is it worth it?'. Evaluation and its link with future planning is a very close one, and one teacher stated that he was 'frequently assessing because it influenced change'.

The overall picture was one of general vagueness. The originally stated aims of the subject were not an integral part of the evaluation procedure apart from skill levels and enjoyment which were referred to at both stages. The major aims of recreation for leisure and health and fitness were only mentioned twice at the evaluation stage. Socialization, which was a very important original aim, did not figure in any of the statements about judging the success of courses. There would certainly appear to be a need for a closer link between the aims of the subject and the manner in which they were evaluated.

Recording individual Progress

Most subject teachers partly record the progress of their pupils by means of numerical or literal grades. These are based on oral or written work, as deemed appropriate, are cumulative throughout the term or year and serve as departmental records. In the sample of physical education teachers interviewed, only three kept a systematic record for each pupil on a card-index filing system. Two had been instituted quite recently as part of the policy of the school and were instigated by the Headmaster. The cards allowed a termly profile to be built up which recorded effort, ability and representative honours. Because the systems were in their infancy, it was not possible to give a reasoned statement as to their effectiveness. Both the teachers were in general approval but stressed the importance of quick and easy recording. Any method that was excessively time consuming was doomed to failure. The third teacher only recorded a physical profile plus representative honours on his system.

Two women teachers kept records in an exercise book but they did not appear to be as comprehensive as the card system. The other eleven teachers did not keep any systematic departmental records and relied upon the school report which was sent out to parents either termly, bi-annually or annually. These reports usually had one or two lines in which comments were written, but occasionally there was complete freedom to write as much as was felt appropriate. The writing of these reports certainly caused some concern because one young teacher said, 'This is the weakest area of what I do. It is all in the head really. We don't grade anything. It is difficult because physical education is so wide'. One school regarded the 'School magazine as the main record' and another kept records of sports results and the names of the pupils who were involved. Two young teachers were considering the institution of a card-index system and the slight conscience about not having already done so was revealed when one said, 'It's something I should possibly do. I have considered it'.

In relation to each individual, the teachers were asked if they recorded progress according to ability and for effort. All, except one, made reference to the importance of recognizing effort in its many forms regardless of ability. Quotations such as, 'We judge on an individual basis and would reward effort', 'Credit for hard work' and 'Effort, approach, application and enthusiasm' tended to be quite typical. One teacher was concerned about being able to recognize effort in all pupils and said, 'For every one I spot, I must miss ten others'. It is certainly easier to assess high attainment, especially when objective criteria are used. Representative honours in school, county and national squads together with high individual achievement were recognized by all and recorded with a great deal of pride. The one exception to recording both ability and effort was not because he regarded one to be more important than the other, but simply because the school report form had allocated one line to physical education and there was no room to record effort.

The overall impression about evaluation in physical education was that a rather unsystematic and vague approach was being used. There were certainly no standardized procedures and the methods used varied with the individual. The compiling of written records was very time consuming and the majority of teachers relied entirely on the school report. The departmental recording systems which were in operation were in their infancy and capable of development.

Reactions of teachers

Content

The question in this section asked if there were any aspects of planning which had been omitted. Most felt that the most important factors were included, but a few additional ones were mentioned. Some of the points had been discussed in some interviews, but because of the partly-structured nature of the discussions might not have been stressed sufficiently. These included:

1 *Financial allocation to the department* Physical education does require a substantial amount of money for the purchase of new, and the upkeep of old, equipment. Also, the transportation of school teams for competitive matches and children to off-site facilities is expensive. Without a sound financial provision, some schools can find their programmes seriously curtailed.

2 *Discipline problems* One teacher was concerned about the disruptive effect some children had upon the programme and this applied particularly to the options courses.

3 *Mixed work* Boys and girls can often be seen working together in the same class in the senior forms of secondary schools in activities like badminton, tennis and swimming. However, it is comparatively rare to

see mixed classes in the first few years and some teachers considered this to be detrimental to their curriculum development.

4 *Developing status of the subject* The statement, 'I would welcome GCE O and A-levels which would put me on an equal status with other subjects' suggested a slight inferiority complex about the value of physical education. CSE Mode III courses were not an acceptable alternative to this teacher as he considered the varying standards rendered them meaningless. This contrasted with other views which expressed full support for the contribution physical education made to the education of children as well as to the life of the school.

5 *Positive support* Implicit in many of the earlier statements has been the importance of positive support from the Headteacher, staff, parents and children, but it was mentioned specifically in this section.

6 *Facilities and timetabling* The provision of adequate facilities and the allocation of a reasonable number of periods on the timetable had been mentioned in earlier discussions, but were again emphasized.

Interview

The teachers were asked to make frank and honest comments on the initial approach, the subsequent letter and the actual conduct of the interview. Some apprehension was expressed by a number of teachers, but most felt that the discussion was a much more pleasant affair than they had expected. As professional physical educationists, most welcomed the opportunity to discuss their work in some detail. Certainly it had made them sit back and reflect on the curriculum they offered to their children and in some cases views had been clarified. Some expressed strong convictions about the values of their work and programmes, whilst others were more tentative. Most were gratified that a research project of this nature should be starting in the schools through discussions with a number of teachers.

It is perhaps important to record the value teachers attached to the discussions amongst themselves and with an outside 'authority' at in-service courses. The more opportunities there are for teachers to express their beliefs and have them criticized in a constructive manner, the more chance there will be for effective curriculum development in the schools.

Summary

The interviews in this first stage of the enquiry have been conducted with a small number of heads of physical education departments from one education authority. In general, all the schools had satisfactory indoor and outdoor facilities and, in some cases, the provision could be described as excellent. Staffing ratios were adequate and most were working in a supportive school and local community environment. The qualifications of the staff were high and their commitment to the children and the subject was to be commended. In broad terms, the sample was possibly biased towards 'good standard' schools. Therefore, the inferences about planning may not necessarily be repeated in a wider national sample.

A number of main points appear to have emerged from the interviews in this sample. These are as follows:

1 Teachers are informal and sometimes even casual in their overall approach to the planning of the curriculum. The written syllabus appears to have a restricted circulation and is rarely made freely available. The suggestion that some guidelines might be forthcoming from the study was welcomed by all the teachers. There certainly seems to be a need for such a framework which would assist teachers in their planning.

2 Teachers appear to have vague ideas concerning the aims and objectives of physical education. In addition, there are also many claims made for the value of the subject particularly by women teachers. It is unacceptable that the objectives and purposes of the various courses are not communicated to the children. The incidental and infrequent nature of any communication that does take place does not suggest clear planning in the initial stages.

3 A common core of work appears to operate during the first three years of the secondary school curriculum. This is then followed by an increasing number of optional activities. Some progressive planning takes place as the children progress through the school, but there is also an indication that there is a considerable amount of intuitive planning, especially in the optional activities programme.

4 The extra-curricular work that is conducted figures prominently in the overall contribution to the work of the department and the life of the school. There are occasions when it seems that this aspect assumes equal if not greater importance than the normal curriculum. However, the general trend suggests that all children, regardless of ability, are welcomed to all extra-curricular activities.

5 There is little evidence that the teachers are making a conscious effort to apply evaluation procedures and they seem to be rather vague and unsystematic in this aspect of curriculum planning. In relation to the monitoring of individual pupils, few departments keep any composite record.

A number of limitations have been exposed in the summary so far, but the overall picture is one of hard work and dedication by a highly motivated group of enthusiastic teachers. Uppermost in the teachers' minds seems to be a need to provide activity and enjoyment for the children. Few would argue that these aspects are desirable ingredients, but the emphasis on the recreational aspects of the subject is an important issue. This is because there is a danger of providing only enjoyable recreative activity and this would represent an unbalanced emphasis as far as curriculum planning in physical education is concerned.

The information from these interviews indicates that the teachers are dedicated and enthusiastic in their work, and have a strong sense of commitment to their subject and the children they teach. However, there would appear to be scope for improvement in the planning procedures they adopt and it is hoped that the information gleaned from these interviews will make a contribution to the research approaches that follow and that some tentative suggestions for planning may emerge.

4 Analyzing the Syllabuses: "We Get Many High Flown Ideas from Books but Physical Education is Mainly Activity".

The second strategy related to planning involved an analysis of a number of physical education syllabuses. The original intention was to collect a sample of syllabuses from secondary schools in England and Wales. The Headteachers of ninety maintained schools received a letter asking them to send a copy of the physical education syllabus with the approval of their head of department. Strict confidentiality was ensured for the name of the school and the identity of the respondents. The sample reflected:

1 Type of school,
2 Sex of school,
3 Region – Registrar General's ten divisions.

Table 3. Syllabus sample by type and sex of school, and region

Number	Type	Sex	Region
30	Secondary Modern	Mixed	3 per region
10	Grammar	Boys	1 per region
10	Grammar	Girls	1 per region
10	Grammar	Mixed	1 per region
30	Comprehensive	Mixed	3 per region

The postal request for syllabuses did not produce the desired information and the response was disappointingly poor. A 22% return produced twenty syllabuses. One can speculate on the reasons for this, but the two most likely ones are that either the written syllabus does not exist in many schools, or that teachers are reluctant to have anyone scrutinize the planning of their courses. This return was similar to that experienced by Jones (1975) in a study of music teachers' attitudes towards the teaching of their subject in secondary schools. This prompted him to say that, 'Most of the teachers did not respond to the request to provide written syllabuses or similar guides to their teaching. This could indicate that their syllabuses are verbally agreed and carried in their heads, or possibly that they work without any kind of syllabus'.

It was abundantly clear that a national sample was not possible. It was therefore decided to make a regional approach through the inspectors and advisers to urban, suburban and rural areas in south-east England. Permission was given to write to eighty-seven schools in these areas. A 20% return resulted in seventeen syllabuses becoming available. In the urban area, ten syllabuses were selected by the adviser without any approach being made to the schools. In terms of statistically random selection procedures this was clearly not acceptable.

To obtain a sample as originally conceived was not possible and the decision was taken that it was better to make an analysis of the available syllabuses rather than abandon the idea altogether. Eventually, forty-seven syllabuses were collected and it was considered desirable to obtain a larger sample. Having decided this, ten syllabuses were made available by a local physical education adviser and five more elicited from teachers in south-west England after an in-service conference. An additional nine syllabuses were collected from teachers at a number of in-service courses conducted by the author. Thus a variety of methods and sources had been used to collect the sample and a summary table of the number and method of obtaining the total sample of seventy-one syllabuses is set out in *Table 4*.

Table 4. Syllabuses: breakdown and method of obtaining sample.

Method		N
Postal request (England and Wales)		20
Postal request (Suburban and Rural)		17
Selected by LEA Adviser (Urban)		10
Selected by LEA Adviser (Suburban and Rural)		10
Postal request (South-west England)		5
In-Service Courses		9
	Total	71

As a result of these varying strategies, these seventy-one syllabuses were subjected to analysis. Eighteen were from boys' schools, twenty-five from girls' schools and twenty-eight from mixed schools. Two analyses were conducted. The purpose of the first analysis was to examine the different aspects which theorists regarded as important in curriculum planning and ascertain the weighting given to aims and objectives, content, teaching method and evaluation. The weighting allocated to these components was made by three independent judges. The second analysis examined the format, presentation and major sections of the syllabuses, and identified those areas considered to be important by practising teachers.

At this point it must be stated that the syllabuses do not represent a national sample and had mainly been obtained from schools in the south of England. Some had been obtained direct from the schools, whereas others had been selected by the advisory staff. This selection procedure would inevitably produce bias, but in spite of these limitations, the sample was considered to be wide enough to make some tentative interpretations.

Analysis 1

Procedure

Three experienced physical educationists (an adviser, a lecturer and a teacher) were approached and asked to give their impressions of the seventy-one syllabuses in the sample. (It is relevant to record that the teacher had earlier been interviewed in the first stage of the enquiry). Each judge worked independently and was given the following information and scoring procedures:

> The following major areas – aims and objectives, content, method and evaluation, are generally recognized as four important factors involved in curriculum planning. You are asked to judge the proportion of each syllabus which is associated with these areas. In order to obtain a qualitative judgement, the proportion that you allocate is to be guided by the emphasis given to the statements as you interpret them rather than to the number of words written. Allocate a total of ten points to each syllabus in proportion to the emphasis associated with each area, *eg*. if a syllabus was equally related to content and method, and no mention was made of the other areas, five points would be allocated to each and you would record as follows:

Syllabus	Aims and Objectives	Content	Method	Evaluation
	0	5	5	0

Approximately half-an-hour was spent with each judge making sure that he understood the instructions and the terminology, as well as rating the first syllabus in the sample. The method outlined above was similar to the procedures used by Taylor (1970), thereby enabling comparisons to be made with analyses of syllabuses for other subjects on the school curriculum.

Results and discussion

Table 5 shows the percentages allocated to each of the four main syllabus components by the three judges for the seventy-one syllabuses in the sample.

Table 5. Percentages allocated by judges to main syllabus components (Analysis 1).

	Aims and Objectives	Content	Method	Evaluation
Adviser	13.7	56	24.7	5.6
Lecturer	15.4	50	25.8	8.8
Teacher	14.7	75.6	8.0	1.7

There is common agreement between the three judges concerning the emphasis given to aims and objectives. In contrast, the teacher rated the proportion associated with content approximately 20 per cent or more higher than the other two judges, and approximately 17 per cent lower in relation to method. In the area of evaluation, the teacher also scored considerably lower. The ratings given by the adviser and lecturer were fairly consistent with each other and did not show any marked variations. The fact that there was a variance between the judges and that the number of judges was small, indicated that the results of this analysis can only suggest trends and general guidelines.

Table 6 shows the above allocation when the percentages are averaged out.

Table 6. Average percentages allocated to main syllabus components.

Aims and Objectives	Content	Method	Evaluation
14.6	60.5	19.5	5.4

By far the largest proportion was linked with the content to be taught in physical education. The least weighting was devoted to evaluation techniques which again tended to support the notion that this was the least sophisticated and articulated part of planning. On average, the judges indicated that forty-four of the syllabuses made no reference to this aspect in any shape or form. The aims and objectives of the subject were stated in some detail in a number of syllabuses and received an average of 15 per cent. However, it is valid to record that the judges, on average, recorded twenty-three syllabuses as having made no statement concerning the aims and objectives of physical education. Teaching methods and advice concerning the different aspects that constitute the subject received a proportion of 19 per cent, but an average of eighteen of the syllabuses made no reference to this area of planning.

The earlier work of Taylor (1970) enabled a comparison to be made with other subject syllabuses and *Table 7* shows the percentage allocations.

Table 7. Average percentages allocated to main syllabus components in Physical Education, English, Geography and Science.

	Aims and Objectives	Content	Method	Evaluation
Physical Education	15	61	19	5
English	14	51	30	5
Geography	6	81	12	1
Science	6	83	9	2

Common with the other three subjects, content received by far the greatest proportion; more so than in English but less than in geography and science. The aims and objectives received a greater emphasis in physical education and English than they did for geography and science. There was far less stress placed on teaching method for physical education than there was for English, but more than for geography and science. Another common factor revealed that evaluation received the lowest proportion in all four subjects.

In summary, the trends indicated by this analysis did not vary to any great extent from the analyses in other subjects. The major impression was that the physical education syllabuses were mainly concerned with statements about content and subject matter, although many made reference to aims and objectives and teaching method. Only a minority of the syllabuses made any reference to evaluation procedures.

Analysis 2

Procedure

An examination of the seventy-one syllabuses by the author of the present study indicated that it would be helpful to structure part of the analysis. Although each syllabus was unique, a number of common factors were apparent. Pre-codings of important areas were taken from the original interviews with the sixteen teachers as well as some post-codings which were determined by inspection of the syllabuses. As a result of this procedure, an analysis sheet was compiled which consisted of introductory factual information about the nature and format of the syllabus and this was followed by twenty-five distinct categories which teachers considered important enough to include. A final section headed 'Comments' enabled any additional factors not included in the above to be added. Each syllabus was analyzed using this sheet (Appendix B) by placing a '√' in the appropriate box. Occasional comments were made against the heading whenever it was considered appropriate. A summary of the complete analysis is shown in *Table 8.*

Table 8. Percentage allocated to main syllabus categories (Analysis 2).

N = 71; Boys = 18; Girls = 25; Boys and Girls = 28.

		%
1	INTRODUCTORY STATEMENT	27
2	STAFF LIST AND QUALIFICATIONS	15
3	JOB SPECIFICATION	3
4	VISITING COACHES	11
5	PROBATIONARY TEACHER GUIDANCE	3
6	STUDENT TEACHER GUIDANCE	3
7	DEPARTMENT MEETINGS	3
8	FINANCE	1
9	FACILITIES	31
10	LISTS OF EQUIPMENT	4
11	CLOTHING	20
12	SHOWERING	13
13	TIME ALLOCATION	58
14	DIAGRAMMATIC PRESENTATION OF SYLLABUS	46
15	COMMON CORE	100
16	OPTIONAL ACTIVITIES	85
17	AWARD SCHEMES	51
18	EXTRA-CURRICULAR ACTIVITIES	39
19	COMPETITION – INTERNAL	37
20	COMPETITION – EXTERNAL	35
21	MEDICAL SERVICE/REMEDIALS	10
22	HEALTH EDUCATION	3
23	SAFETY	25
24	AUDIO-VISUAL AIDS	7
25	BIBLIOGRAPHY	4

Format

The first and most obvious difference was the enormous variation in size. This variation ranged from two syllabuses which were incorporated into a written letter to a typewritten one of ninety pages in length. Four were under three hundred words in length and one was a diagrammatic representation of activity emphasis each term. Sixty of the seventy-one syllabuses were typewritten and reproduced on a duplicating machine. One was professionally printed and this certainly provided a very high standard of presentation. The general impression created was that most were satisfactory. There were only a few that were of a poor standard.

Only three syllabuses had a cover page incorporating the name of the school and a design appropriate to physical activity. An occasional colour code was used to differentiate between different sections of the syllabus and although this was a rarity, it did help ease of reference. Several numbered the pages in a logical order, but sometimes sections had been added and this created some problems in terms of logical numerical progression. Very few prefaced the syllabus with a contents page in spite of the fact that the majority formulated their statements under major headings or categories.

There is no doubt that some teachers had given a lot of thought to the presentation and content of their syllabus, whereas others had written it out in order to meet the request of this study. However, the returns appeared to be a fair representation of the work done in the schools. The fact that there was a high nil return from the schools, coupled with enormous variety in standard of presentation, seems to support the notion that teachers have considerable differences of opinion regarding the importance of the written syllabus. It is also apparent that not all members of the profession consider it to be part of their responsibility to produce a written physical education syllabus.

Another fact that emerged was that there was considerable difference of opinion over exactly what was meant by a syllabus. Many included statements about aims and content, and when certain activities should be taught. All the longer syllabuses incorporated a 'syllabus' for activities such as athletics, dance, gymnastics and a variety of games. Some teachers regarded these as schemes of work rather than part of the formal syllabus for the subject.

Introductory statement

Of the 27 per cent who included some kind of introduction to the syllabus, the majority related to the virtues and justifications of physical education. Only rarely was there a statement which said anything about the background and situation of the school or its social and environmental setting. Most did not consider an introduction necessary and usually began with either a statement of aims or a statement concerning content.

Staff: Qualifications and job specification

Comparatively few (15 per cent) regarded a list of the staff and their qualifications to be worthy of inclusion. Usually there was merely a mention of the number and sex of teachers working in the department on a full or part-time basis. However, there were two instances where the duties and responsibilities of the staff were itemized. Details such as teaching load, responsibilities for areas of work, school teams, extra-curricular activities and administrative duties were included.

Visiting coaches

The use of visiting coaches by physical education departments to supplement the range of options that is offered has been a popular and often worthwhile addition to the curriculum in recent years. In the present sample of syllabuses, 11 per cent acknowledged the fact that they employed additional coaches using on or off-site facilities. Usually, it was associated with the option programme that was offered to pupils in the senior part of the school. Reference was made in a few instances to screening procedures by either the local authority or physical education advisers before coaches could be approached to teach children in educational institutions.

Probationary teacher and student guidance

Two schools (3 per cent) considered it necessary to specify in some detail items that teachers should observe. These ranged from preparation of work to general organization and administration. The probationary teacher guidance was directed to normal daily routines, availability of assistance, personal involvement and teaching development, whereas the second category consisted of advice and instructions to staff when there were teacher training students working within the department.

Department meetings

There were only two instances (3 per cent) where mention was made of meetings for the department. In one case they were held once a month and 'whenever it is felt desirable' and in the other the meetings were held weekly. The acceptance of department or faculty meetings has been stressed in school organization over recent years, but this sample of syllabuses from the 1970s certainly did not reflect this trend. However, it may well be that the heads of department did not consider it necessary to refer to meetings in a syllabus outline.

Finance

In times of constantly rising prices and inflation, it was surprising that only one school felt it worth including a section on finance within the syllabus and actually specified the amount of money that was allocated. The high cost of sporting equipment coupled with travelling costs to and from inter-school matches prove a constant source of concern to physical education departments. This particular school was investigating ways of raising additional money through subscriptions, contributions and sponsorship from local firms.

Facilities

All physical education departments have indoor and outdoor facilities at their disposal. These vary enormously from those who have to share school halls and use playgrounds, to others with purpose built sports halls and swimming pools. Thirty-one per cent of the syllabuses included a list of the facilities and in a few instances diagrams were included to show the layout of fields in summer and winter. Quite a high proportion utilized off-site facilities and there appeared to be two main reasons for this. One was because the facilities did not exist on site, *eg*. playing fields and swimming baths in dense urban areas, and the second was related to the increase in the range of options offered to senior pupils which could often only be achieved by this means, *eg*. squash courts and ice-skating rinks.

Lists of equipment

To make lists of all the equipment used by a department would clearly be inappropriate and would only duplicate the records that are made in the stock books. However, 4 per cent of the syllabuses did include details of the larger pieces of apparatus, but these were in relation to fixed and portable gymnastic equipment.

Clothing

All physical education teachers should be concerned that children participate in a variety of physical activities wearing appropriate clothing. Fourteen schools (20 per cent) made specific reference to this either by directly specifying the type of shoes and colour of clothing to be worn or by indirectly referring to attire suitable to the activity.

Showering

To take a shower after a period of vigorous activity is normal hygienic practice. However, one of the concerns in many schools is that by the time children have arrived at the place of activity, changed into kit, showered and changed back into their normal clothes, there is very little time left to partake in the actual activity. The only 'time saver' in this routine is to miss out the shower and there is no doubt that many schools do. In this sample, 13 per cent considered it important enough to write into their syllabus that children would be expected to shower at the end of every lesson.

Time allocation

The amount of time allocated to physical education on the school timetable for each year is an integral part of the planning of any course. In view of this fact, it is rather surprising that only 58 per cent included it in their syllabus. The general trend showed that fewer periods were allocated to physical education the longer the child was at school and this tends to substantiate the earlier findings of Kane (1974). In only a few instances was the total syllabus subjected to a 'time analysis' which indicated the amount of time allocated to the variety of activities that constituted physical education.

Diagrammatic presentation

A diagrammatic representation of the syllabus gives a quick impression of the activities included in the programme as well as an indication of the term and year in which they are to be taught. For some, diagrams of this nature represented the total syllabus without any additions, whereas others included it as part of their total presentation. Regardless of its position in relation to other planning components, 46 per cent chose to use diagrams to present their syllabus wholly or partially.

Common core and optional activities

Most schools nowadays operate a system in physical education which insists that all children follow a basic course for two, three or four years. This is followed by some limited choices before there is finally a free choice from a large range of options. Without exception, every school in this sample believed that children should be exposed to a common core of activities which generally comprised athletics, major games, gymnastics, swimming and dance (for girls). The emphasis and range varied slightly according to the staffing, facilities and philosophy of the school. Optional activities were specifically mentioned in 85 per cent of the syllabuses. To say that the other 15 per cent did not have options would not necessarily be true. It may have been that they had not been included in the written presentation.

It was apparent that teachers placed greater emphasis on stating objectives in the overt areas to the exclusion of the covert aspects. For example, the planning of objectives was specified more clearly in games and athletics than it was in educational gymnastics where the planning was less specific and much more broadly based.

Award schemes

The merits of using the variety of award schemes available in the physical education programme is a contentious issue amongst teachers. Some regard them as taking up too much teaching time and feel that they should not be part of the lesson. Others consider them to act as strong motivators and provide children and teachers with objective measures of evaluation. Certainly the badges and certificates that are awarded are valued by the children. The analysis seemed to reflect this division of opinion as 51 per cent made reference to the use of award schemes and it was usually incorporated into the contents section of specific areas of work. The Five Star Athletic, and Swimming Survival and Life Saving awards were by far the most commonly mentioned. Other activities included hockey and netball umpiring, trampolining, gymnastics and Duke of Edinburgh awards in outdoor activities. Some schools referred to one award scheme being incorporated into the programme whereas others mentioned as many as seven.

Extra-curricular activities

Nearly all physical education departments run an active programme of clubs and team practices during the lunch hour, after school and at weekends. This additional voluntary work is expected of any self-respecting department. These are occasions which provide enjoyment for large numbers of children. The practice sessions also provide opportunity to develop high levels of skill. They are valued by staff and children, and often bring prestige to the school through representative honours. It was therefore surprising to find that only 39 per cent considered them worthy of mention. Usually they were headed as a separate section but it was not uncommon to find them incorporated with other areas.

Competition: internal and external

Thirty-seven per cent referred to internal and 35 per cent to external competition. Again, it was surprising that just over one-third of the sample incorporated the organized competitive sport of the school into their syllabuses. Some of the arrangements for internal competitions were quite elaborate and specified them in considerable detail. The House system was frequently mentioned and the range of activities involved. Competition with other schools invariably revolved round the games teams at all levels within the locality of the school. However, several syllabuses referred to competitions, such as rugby tours, which took place further afield.

Medical service and remedials

This section was very much a mixture of headings that could loosely be called ''medical', and details ranged from first aid facilities to work with remedial classes. One school placed a non-swimmers club into this category, while another hoped that members of the physical education department would help to teach hand-eye co-ordination, improve postural defects and generally give assistance in this area as required. A card-index on every child who had any physical or mental disability was noted in one syllabus. Only 10 per cent of the sample made reference to medical services and remedial work, and this was usually just one or two sentences.

Health Education

'Health education is part of physical education' is a phrase that is often used. As a practical subject, physical education has a direct bearing on issues that are of major concern in present Western society. These issues include diet, smoking, drugs and stress. A fuller understanding of these topics can develop through their relationship with physical activity. Whether health education should be an incidental part of physical education, or alternatively a separately taught course, is a debatable point. As far as this sample went, only 3 per cent specifically referred to health education and then it was only taught on an irregular basis during wet weather programmes. It was not felt to be of sufficient importance to replace the normal practical activities.

Safety

The application of the Health and Safety at Work Act to education has made us all aware of the responsibilities we have towards children, and this is particularly so in physical education where there are many potential hazards in the use of equipment and the natural environment. Pamphlets on safety procedures in a variety of activities are published, but were rarely mentioned. Generally, safety referred to activities such as throwing in athletics, life-saving in swimming and supporting in both gymnastics and trampolining. Only 25 per cent of the syllabuses made any reference to safety.

Audio-visual aids

The so-called technological age does not appear to have had a great deal of impact on physical education. Seven per cent of the sample referred to the occasional film for basketball or life-saving. Loops and wall charts had a passing reference and one school wrote about the importance of a Sports Notice Board. Sophisticated procedures such as video tape recording and filming were not mentioned and it is reasonable to assume there is limited use made of this kind of technology in modern physical education departments.

Bibliography

Four per cent of the syllabuses included lists of books that would be helpful to teachers, but only one could be described as being comprehensive. The remainder just made passing reference to the titles of books at the end of a syllabus for a particular activity. Usually they were available in the school library but one department kept their own books in order that they would be readily available for staff to consult.

Additional comments

A number of other factors were considered to be important enough to incorporate into the written syllabus of one or two schools. These included:

1 *Ability grouping* Grouping children by physical ability is not uncommon in physical education. This is particularly true in extra-curricular activities where the squad system is in operation. In the ordinary lesson, the children are not streamed and attend in their normal classroom group. However, it should be noted that it is possible to stream within this structure and in reality, this occurs quite frequently.

2 *Certificate of Secondary Education* Many schools are now incorporating a Mode III syllabus into their curriculum in the fourth and fifth years. This necessitates a full and detailed syllabus presentation and the guarantee of a time allocation of at least four periods a week for two years. In schools where the CSE has been initiated, the written documentation formed part of the total syllabus.

3 *Co-educational work* Opportunities for boys and girls to work together were usually offered in the optional activities programme in the upper school. Occasional reference was made to co-educational work being conducted in dance and educational gymnastics in the first year.

4 *Future development* An appraisal of some of the major problems encountered and how the department could develop in the future were considered to be important by some teachers. There is no doubt that forward and creative thinking of this nature could influence Headteachers' plans for future development within schools.

5 *Ground staff* No physical education department operates effectively without the co-operation of the ground staff and the role they play is an important one.

6 *School teams and sporting events* Sections were occasionally devoted to the values of school teams and the areas in which they operated. Sometimes they were linked to visits to national and local sporting events.

7 *Wet weather programme* Most games programmes rely on reasonable weather conditions, but the inclusion of suggestions for alternatives during inclement weather is a worthwhile contribution.

Summary

The analysis of the seventy-one syllabuses in this study showed that only four categories were recorded by more than half the sample. Three of these related to content and comprised the common core of work, optional activities and the use of award schemes. The other category referred to the amount of time allocated to physical education in the total curriculum. It appears that all schools insist on a compulsory common core of work in the first few years of secondary education, with the vast majority incorporating an optional activities system in the upper school. This area of content includes the substantial use of award schemes in the curriculum, as just over half the sample considered them important enough to include in the written syllabus. As the children progressed through the school, the general trend of time allocation indicated a reduction in the number of periods allocated to physical education.

Between approximately a third and a half referred to the importance of extra-curricular activities as well as internal and external competition. Much of this work takes place outside the normal time-tabled hours but is an integral part of all physical education departments. It was rather surprising that such an important aspect of the curriculum was not included in the majority of syllabuses. Facilities also figured in this percentage category with lists of on and off-site facilities available. A diagrammatic representation of the syllabus can give a quick insight into the number of activities included in the programme and when they should be taught. Nearly half used this method of presentation and for some it represented the total syllabus.

There were a few categories which were used by approximately a quarter of the sample. These included introductory statements relating to the virtues and justification of physical education in the curriculum, but rarely was there any information about the school, its population and the social and environmental background. Comparatively few syllabuses regarded a list of staff, their qualifications and responsibilities worthy of inclusion. It appears that a statement about safety factors – an area of paramount importance for physical education teachers – was included in only a quarter of the syllabuses. It was surprising that some of the excellent pamphlets published on this aspect were hardly mentioned.

In addition, there were a number of other categories such as visiting coaches, equipment, showering, medical and audio-visual aids which were mentioned in a minority of syllabuses.

A disturbing aspect was the high nil return from the schools in the initial sample. Although one cannot be certain of the reasons for this, it is not unreasonable to speculate that many heads of department do not consider it part of their professional responsibility to write a syllabus for the physical education of the children in their schools. As a number of syllabuses were sent direct from the advisory staff, they had already been sifted to some extent, making the ones that were analyzed a biased sample towards the better presented documents. If this was the case, then there can be no complacency over this particular aspect of planning in physical education.

There is no doubt that physical education departments do many things which they do not include in their written syllabus. This lack of documentation is a pity, because the picture which emerges is not a true reflection of the work that is actually taking place. The content of the subject appears to dominate nearly all the presentations, with evaluation receiving the least emphasis. The main headings for each syllabus varied from school to school, but not one used aims and objectives, content, teaching methods and evaluation which are the four most commonly identified aspects of curriculum planning. These results are similar to other analyses conducted with academic subjects. In summary, the analysis of this sample suggested that something is left to be desired in relation to the content and presentation of many of the syllabuses. Teachers are unsure how to present their work in the form of a written syllabus and there would appear to be some support for the earlier contention that they might find guidelines helpful in the planning of the physical education curriculum.

5 Responses to the Questionnaire – a National Perspective: "This is the Only Syllabus I Have Ever Seen. The Headmaster Probably Hasn't Seen It".

The interviews with heads of physical education departments, the analyses of syllabuses and the review of literature had revealed a number of important factors and issues regarding curriculum content and curriculum planning. From the small sample of interviews it was not clear how important teachers regarded these factors and issues in relation to their physical education planning. One way to ascertain their importance was to construct a questionnaire for a national survey using the preliminary information as a foundation. This would add objectivity to the study and give a sound basis on which to explore some of the unresolved questions. Basically there were seven questions. These were:

1 Which staff are involved in planning?
2 When is the planning done?
3 Which factors influence planning?
4 What methods are used in planning?
5 What is the purpose of planning?
6 How is the planning communicated?
7 How is the success of the planning judged?

In the questionnaire, these represented separate sections which were preceded by biographical information about the teachers and their schools. A short statement about the issues to be probed in the seven main sections is set out in the following paragraphs.

Staff involvement in planning It was evident that many staff were involved in the planning of courses and that their role and importance varied considerably. Not only were the full-time physical education staff involved but so also were full-time academic staff who taught some occasional periods. In any kind of dynamic curriculum there are bound to be changes and the manner in which these changes were implemented was probed.

Timing of planning Departmental meetings were held formally and frequently in some schools whereas in others they were quite informal and intermittent. This led to the formulation of questions which investigated this particular area. The manner in which departmental policies were formulated varied greatly.

Influencing factors There were obviously many factors which influenced the planning of the physical education curriculum and the importance that was attached to any one factor varied from school to school. A number of influencing factors, based on interviews, analysis and literature review, were listed and the teachers asked to record the importance they attached to each factor on a 5 point scale which ranged from 'very important' to 'not important at all'. A common core of work was frequently mentioned during the interviews and incorporated into some syllabuses. Confirmation of this trend was considered worthwhile.

Method of planning It was abundantly clear that teachers would appreciate guidelines for their planning. The written syllabuses that had been analyzed earlier in the study revealed a number of deficiencies and it was decided to probe areas such as who was involved in planning and how strategies were formulated.

Purpose of planning Aims and objectives, content, method and evaluation are generally recognized as four important factors in curriculum planning. The emphasis that is placed in each area will vary and this led to the formulation of a quantitative judgement on each of the four main factors. Additionally, a list of the purposes that the curriculum might serve was compiled and the teachers asked to rate the degree of importance of each item.

Communication From the interviews it was apparent that teachers did not communicate their long-term aims to children and that this also applied to the communication of shorter-term objectives. It was evident that the methods of communicating the curriculum plan to colleagues who taught physical education and the assurance of its implementation varied considerably.

Evaluation It was clear that teachers used a number of criteria to judge the efficiency of their physical education programmes and that these did not always correlate with the original aims stated in the interviews. Again, teachers were asked to rate the degree of importance for each method of evaluation on a 5 point scale. The manner in which teachers recorded pupils' progress was also investigated.

Preliminary survey

Initially the questionnaire was given to three colleagues who were experienced physical education lecturers with substantial teaching experience. The purposes of this initial pilot survey were first, to remove some of the more obvious flaws and secondly, to discuss the reasoning behind the questionnaire. After completion, the three staff engaged me in a frank and forthright discussion about the purpose and presentation of the survey. As a result, a number of additions, deletions and alterations were made which gave greater clarity and removed ambiguities. Subsequently, the questionnaire was discussed with three University lecturers in Education who made many critically constructive comments which were implemented. The format was arranged to allow the data to be processed by computer.

Pilot survey

The questionnaire was completed and sent to the heads of physical education departments in 38 schools in five authorities which were not involved in the main sample. As far as possible, the pilot sample reflected the type, size and sex of schools that were to be used in the main study. Thirty-two schools returned the questionnaire which resulted in a response of 84 per cent. The pilot survey proved to be most useful for the following reasons:

1 it eliminated unclear and ambiguous phrases,
2 it enabled errors to be identified in the data coding process,
3 the complete questionnaire was exposed to physical education teachers,
4 the teachers were asked to make comments and some did in considerable detail.

There were three multiple type questions which required a larger pilot sample in order to test the internal consistency and run a factor analysis on the preliminary data. An additional forty copies of these questions were sent to schools in four authorities which were not involved in the main sample. Thirty-four returns were received which reflected a response rate of 85 per cent. As a result of this pilot testing, the level of internal consistency for each of the three questions was found to be satisfactory and the factor analysis indicated that some meaningful data might be revealed.

The final version of the questionnaire is to be found in Appendix C.

The sample

A total sample of 793 schools were approached in ten authorities in England and Wales*. All the schools included in the sample were secondary schools with intakes at 11, 12 or 13 years. A two-way stratification was used according to:

*The Central Research Funds Committee, University of London, awarded a grant towards the cost of the questionnaire.

1 Region: North, South-East, East, West, Midlands and Wales.
2 Type of School: Comprehensive, Grammar, Secondary Modern/High.

A breakdown of the sample by region and type of school is shown in *Table 9*.

Table 9. Total sample by region and type of school

Region	Authority	Grammar	Comprehensive	Sec.Modern/ High	Totals
North	Cumbria	8	41	11	60 = 182
	Lancashire	10	86	26	122
South-East	Kent	32	37	78	147
East	Essex	12	87	11	110 = 180
	Lincolnshire	16	18	36	70
West	Devon	16	36	28	80 = 127
	Dorset	11	22	14	47
Midlands	Staffordshire	3	79	9	91
Wales	Clwyd	0	31	0	31 = 66
	Dyfed	4	25	6	35
	Totals	112	462	219	793

The Chief Education Officer of each authority was approached to ask for permission to invite the secondary schools in their county to take part in the research project. A copy of the proposed questionnaire was sent with the request. Every authority agreed to the schools being approached on the clear understanding that it was for individual schools to decide whether or not to complete the survey. The Headteacher of each of the 793 schools was written to inviting his school to participate in the project. A letter was also written to the head of physical education asking him to complete the questionnaire. A brief background to the study was included as it was felt that this would be helpful in setting the scene and encouraging a response. A copy of the questionnaire and a Freepost envelope for the return were also enclosed. For those schools who did not reply, a first reminder and a further copy of the questionnaire was sent out after an interval of two months. A second reminder was sent to non-responding schools one month later. Returns were received from 608 schools out of the total sample of 793 as follows:

1st request ... 452 replies ... 57 per cent return
2nd request ... 123 replies ... 16 per cent return
3rd request ... 33 replies ... 4 per cent return
Totals: 608 replies ... 77 per cent return

Table 10. Sample: returns by region and type of school.

Region	Authority	GRAMMAR		COMPREHENSIVE		SEC.MOD/HIGH		TOTAL	
		Sample	Replies	Sample	Replies	Sample	Replies	Sample	Replies
North	Cumbria	8	6	41	26	11	6	60	38
	Lancashire	10	9	86	63	26	21	122	93
South-East	Kent	32	30	37	35	78	72	147	137
East	Essex	12	9	37	62	11	10	110	81
	Lincolnshire	16	11	18	12	36	24	70	47
West	Devon	16	14	36	27	28	17	80	58
	Dorset	11	10	22	18	14	13	47	41
Midlands	Staffordshire	3	2	79	58	9	8	91	68
Wales	Clwyd	0	0	31	24	0	0	31	24
	Dyfed	4	0	25	18	6	3	35	21
	Totals	112	91	462	343	219	174	793	608

The above totals include 36 replies (4.5 per cent) which did not complete the questionniare. The majority of these stated that they did not wish to participate in the project, whilst others gave reasons such as amalgamation, pending closure, illness of staff and pressure of work.

In view of the impersonal nature of mailed questionnaires in a national survey, a response rate of 77 per cent was considered to be satisfactory. A breakdown of response rate by region and type of school was undertaken to see if any of the stratification or the individual cells had received a poor response. The detailed analysis is set out in *Table 10*.

When the raw data of *Table 10* is converted to percentages, the following results appear in *Table 11*.

Table 11. Sample: percentage returns by region and type of school

Region	Authority	Grammar % return	Comprehensive % return	S.M./High % return	Totals % return
North	Cumbria Lancashire	75 90 – 83	63 73 – 70	55 81 – 73	63 76 – 72
South-East	Kent	94	95	92	93
East	Essex Lincolnshire	75 69 – 71	71 67 – 70	91 67 – 72	74 67 – 71
West	Devon Dorset	88 91 – 89	75 82 – 78	61 93 – 71	73 87 – 78
Midlands	Staffordshire	67	73	89	75
Wales	Clwyd Dyfed	– 0	77 72 – 75	– 50	77 60 – 68
	Totals % return	81	74	79	77

A breakdown of the percentage response rate for each region is shown in *Table 12*.

Table 12. Percentage response rate by region

Region	Response rate
North	72%
South-East	93%
East	71%
West	78%
Midlands	75%
Wales	68%

With two exceptions, the total percentage response rates were in the seventies and this was considered satisfactory for the purposes of the analysis. One exception, Wales, was slightly below this (68 per cent) and the other exception, the South-East, was well in excess (93 per cent). The latter may be accounted for by the fact that the author worked in the area and had conducted a number of in-service courses within the authority. The returns for Wales showed 45 responses from a possible 66 and although this indicated a 68 per cent return, the actual number of schools participating was not great. The breakdown of the response in this region will be considered later as two of the cells indicated very poor returns.

The percentage response rate for each type of school is shown in *Table 13*.

Table 13. Percentage response rate by type of school

Type of School	Response rate
Comprehensive	74%
Grammar	81%
Secondary Modern/High	79%

All three returns were considered to be satisfactory. There were 343 Comprehensive, 91 Grammar and 174 Secondary Modern/High schools who participated in the survey. The number of grammar schools is smaller in comparison to the other two types of school, but this reflected the trend in the national distribution.

Not all the schools who replied completed the questionnaire and *Table 14* indicates the numbers and type of school who did complete the survey.

Table 14. Completed questionnaire returns by type of school

Type of School	Replies	Replies with completed questionnaire
Comprehensive	343	315
Grammar	91	85
Sec.Mod/High	174	172
	N = 608	N = 572

Response rate in individual cells

Column totals on the two-way stratification by region and type of school can often hide important information contained in individual cells in the matrix. Visual inspection identified a number of cells which had received a slightly lower than average response rate. In the north, Cumbria had recorded an overall response rate of 63 per cent. This was compiled from returns of 75 per cent for grammar schools, 63 per cent for comprehensive schools and 55 per cent for secondary modern/high schools. In the last category, six of the eleven schools had replied and this accounted for the comparatively low return of 55 per cent.

In the east, all the percentage returns for Lincolnshire were in the high sixties. The same statement can also be made about the grammar school return from Staffordshire in the Midlands, but in terms of actual numbers, two out of three were completed. The only cell to fall short in the west was the secondary modern/high schools return of 61 per cent for Devon. In Wales, two cells in Dyfed showed returns of 0 per cent for grammar (nil return from 4) and 50 per cent for secondary modern/high schools (3 returns from 6). The remaining 19 cells recorded returns between 71 per cent and 95 per cent.

In summary, the overall response of 77 per cent was considered to be satisfactory for this type of mailed questionnaire. Even when the replies which had not completed the questionnaire were subtracted, a return of 72 per cent still regarded as satisfactory. Additionally, the response by region and type of school also reached acceptable levels. However, two cells were resistant to the survey, namely the grammar and secondary modern high schools in Dyfed, but it was recognized from the outset that the number of schools in these categories was low.

Overall, 23 per cent of the schools did not reply and it is pertinent to ask the reasons for this non-response. An indication can be elicited from the replies of schools who wrote declining to complete the questionnaire. By far the most common reasons were that, either the schools were being inundated with requests to participate in research projects and could not cope with any more surveys or that the staff were too heavily pressured by work. In all probability these were also valid reasons for the non-response schools. The timing of the despatch of the questionnaire deliberately avoided the beginning and end of the academic year which are notoriously busy times for physical education teachers. March was, therefore, felt to be a good month when inclement weather might offer staff the opportunity to make a return. The reminders in May and June were perhaps not ideal times for making this kind of request.

The length of the questionnaire is an important factor that will affect the response rate and there can be no denying that the questionnaire in this survey was long. It extended to 13 pages and, in spite of a simplified presentation that required a tick for an answer, would have taken half-an-hour to complete. This may well have been a factor which contributed to non-participation.

The immediate or even long-term value that physical education teachers gain from participating in research studies is not readily obvious and this would certainly have affected their attitude to the request. In this instance, the initial links with teachers at 'grass roots' level was stressed and how this had been influential in the formulation of the questionnaire. A commitment to make the information available through publications and in-service courses was given in the correspondence which may have gone part-way to explain the link that was being attempted between curriculum theory and practice in physical education.

It was clearly stated on the first page of the questionnaire that all the answers would be treated confidentially and that neither the name of the school nor the identity of the respondents would be revealed to anyone in any way. Whilst I am sure this would have been accepted by all the teachers, there may have been a slight feeling of uncertainty in some minds that a researcher had a record about the planning and implementation of the physical education curriculum in their school.

Would the replies of the non-respondents have been markedly different from the actual sample who did reply? This is an impossible question to answer but it is conceivable that they could have affected the distribution of replies. However, this is an imponderable and the analysis had to be made on the available data which, as stated previously, was considered to be acceptable.

Information about the teachers and the schools

The first section of the questionnaire elicited certain biographical information about the teachers and the type of schools in which they taught. The majority of replies (73 per cent) were received from men teachers and it appeared that there are many more men than women who are appointed as heads of department. The exact ages of the teachers were not recorded, but the age range and the length of specialist physical education teaching indicated a wide cross-section from probationary teachers in their first year to a very experienced teacher with forty years teaching service. The majority were in the 31–40 years age bracket but 34 per cent of the sample had achieved head of department status by the age of 30 years. There was certainly a heavy bias towards the younger end of the age range which suggests that physical education teachers achieve promotion quite early in their careers.

The types of school had been prespecified in the original sampling and reflected Comprehensive, Grammar and Secondary Modern/High schools. More than half of the sample were Comprehensive schools with a small group (15 per cent) of Grammar schools. Over three-quarters of the schools were mixed (boys and girls) and where there was a mixed physical education department, a male teacher was usually in charge (85 per cent). The size of the school varied from the smallest secondary school, with 160 pupils, to the largest comprehensive school, with 2,650 pupils. The majority of schools (63 per cent) had under 1,000 pupils on roll.

In total, a wide variety of men and women teachers with a varied background of experience of specialist physical education teaching had responded to the survey from three different types of school. The schools themselves also varied considerably in size from very small to very large.

Heads of departments (N=572)

The replies from the sample were distributed as indicated in *Table 15*.

Table 15. Heads of Department

Type of Department	N	%
Head of Boys' PE	188	33
Head of Girls' PE	117	20
Head of Boys' & Girls' PE	267	47

Sex of teachers

Respondents were asked to indicate their sex and *Table 16* summarizes the results.

Table 16. Sex of teachers

Sex of respondent	N	%
Male	416	73
Female	156	27

By a process of simple addition and subtraction between and within the above two tables, it appeared that where the boys' and girls' physical education departments in 267 schools were amalgamated, there were 228 males and 39 females in charge.

Age range of teachers

The exact age of the teacher was not asked for, but each teacher was asked to indicate the age range to which they belonged in ten-year intervals.

Table 17. Age range of teachers

Age Range	N	%
21–30 years	195	34
31–40 years	254	44
41–50 years	96	17
Over 50 years	27	5

Length of physical education teaching

The length of time that each respondent had been employed as a specialist physical education teacher was recorded in years. In order to condense and simplify the results, *Table 18* summarizes the data in intervals of five years.

Table 18. Length of physical education teaching

Length of teaching service	N	%
1–5 years	67	12
6–10 years	203	35
11–15 years	149	26
16–20 years	76	13
21–25 years	43	8
Over 25 years	34	6

The range of teaching experience extended from one teacher in his first year of teaching to another in his fortieth year of service. The average length of teaching was 12 years and the sum of all the years teaching in the sample amounted to 7,122 years.

Type of school

The types of school were identified in the original sample, *ie.* Comprehensive, Grammar or Secondary Modern/High. The distribution is summarized in *Table 19.*

Table 19. Type of School

Type of School	N	%
Comprehensive	315	55
Grammar	85	15
Secondary Modern/High	172	30

Size of school

The schools ranged in size from the smallest with 160 pupils to the largest Comprehensive with a roll of 2,650 pupils. Again, the information is condensed into intervals in *Table 20.*

Table 20. Size of School

Size of school	N	%
Under 500 pupils	78	13
500–999 pupils	285	50
1,000–1,499 pupils	168	29
1,500–1,999 pupils	39	7
Over 1,999 pupils	2	1

Single sex or mixed school

The majority of schools in the sample were mixed schools and *Table 21* indicates the distribution between single sex and mixed schools.

Table 21. Single sex or mixed schools

School	N	%
Boys	64	11
Girls	60	11
Mixed	448	78

The above seven variables, together with the six regions, were used to elicit more detailed information concerning the responses to a number of questions in later sections of the questionnaire. The variables were named as follows:

Region
Head of Department
Sex of teacher
Age of teacher
Length of teaching
Type of school
Size of school
Single sex or mixed school

Staff involvement

The second section of the questionnaire was concerned with the part played by the staff in the planning of the physical education curriculum.

Head of department

The first question asked the heads of department to indicate the part that they played in the planning of courses. *Table 22* summarizes the results.

Table 22. Head of department: involvement in planning

Involvement in planning	%
Major part	90
Moderate part	7
Minor part	3

It was to be expected that the vast majority of teachers with the responsibility of organizing and running a department would have a major role to play in the planning stages. The above data supported this contention, but it was surprising that 10 per cent of the heads of department felt that they only played either a moderate or minor part in planning.

Staff involvement in planning

Two questions were posed to ascertain how much full-time staff in the physical education department and full-time academic staff who taught some physical education were involved in planning.

Table 23. Planning involvement of full-time PE staff and academic staff teaching some PE

Planning involvement	Full-time PE staff. %	Academic staff teaching some PE %
A great deal	54	4
Often	32	13
Occasionally	11	35
Rarely	2	25
Never	1	23

It is to be expected that the full-time staff would play a substantial role in planning, and 86 per cent were centrally involved in this aspect of the curriculum process. This contrasted with the lesser degree of involvement by full-time academic staff who taught some physical education. Ideally, all full-time physical education staff should take part in all aspects of planning. In this way they can feel they have been involved and consulted, and that the final plan has evolved through a democratic process. It would be unrealistic to involve academic staff in the total physical education plan, but it is not unrealistic, and may well be advisable, to incorporate their ideas into the planning of those aspects of the curriculum which they teach. This would not appear to be the case in most instances in the present sample.

Curriculum change

There will always be changes in any curriculum which may or may not be outside the control of the staff. Issues such as finance, facilities, timetable allocation and content are but a few examples. When these changes do occur, they can have an effect on the manner in which the curriculum is implemented. Question 11 attempted to ascertain the way in which changes were made.

Table 24. *Curriculum change*

Curriculum change	% Yes	% No
Imposed by head of dept.	35	65
Through departmental meetings	63	37
Through informal discussion	61	39

The results indicated that 65 per cent of heads of department do not impose change. Where change was imposed, there were indications through written comments on the questionnaire that the imposition was carried out by the heads of department as part of their responsibility after consultation had taken place with their colleagues.

Departmental meetings were held in 63 per cent of the schools as a means of discussing changes in the curriculum. Physical education staff teach in close proximity to one another which makes informal discussion much easier than in many other subjects and 61 per cent used this as an opportunity to implement change.

Column totals in *Table 24* added up to more than 100 per cent which indicated the three methods were not discrete and that a combination of methods was used. A more detailed analysis showed that seventy-eight schools (14 per cent) used all three methods for implementing change as opposed to six schools (1 per cent) who used none of these methods. The most common approach was through departmental meetings or informal discussion, or a combination of these. Only forty-four heads of department (8 per cent) stated that they imposed change without any form of consultation.

Apart from the three methods suggested, 3 per cent of the teachers indicated alternatives. These were concerned with either enforced change through time-tabling or lack of facilities imposed by the Headteacher, or an intrinsic need for change within the department brought about by staff evaluation or ideas from in-service courses.

Place of physical education in the school curriculum

The place of any subject in the school curriculum is the responsibility of the Headteacher. Responses suggested that the Headteacher (37 per cent) or in consultation with the Deputy Head (22 per cent) were mainly responsible. In 39 per cent of the sample, the Headteacher consulted with heads of department (35 per cent) and with the full staff (4 per cent). The information supported the notion of senior staff in the school having the biggest influence in consulting the Headteacher about the place of physical education in the school curriculum. A small group (2 per cent) adopted alternative methods such as faculty meetings, timetable committees and curriculum planning councils.

The responses to the questions in the section on staff involvement indicated a high degree of participation by full-time staff. However, for academic staff who taught some physical education, the reverse was the case. Where changes were necessary, very few heads of department imposed the change without some form of prior consultation. Again, this supports the contention of democratic procedures being used within the departments. In theory, all staff who teach physical education should be consulted during the planning stage. Ultimately, it is the responsibility of the head of department and it is inconceivable that he should not be centrally involved at all times. In the main, an 'open' system of planning and consultation emerged, but there were areas that might have benefitted from even more staff involvement.

Timing of planning

Most physical education departments hold meetings at various points throughout the academic year and Questions 13, 14 and 15 attempted to ascertain the regularity, time and format of these meetings.

Regularity of meetings

Table 25 summarizes the regularity of department meetings.

Table 25. Regularity of department meetings

Regularity of meeting	%
Weekly	11
Monthly	13
Termly	19
Annually	2
Seldom	3
Never	3
As required	49

Of the regular meetings, termly was the most common, although substanial numbers were holding meetings on either a weekly or monthly basis. The 'Seldom' and 'Never' categories received a 6 per cent response which indicated that a considerable number of departments rarely met. This may be partly accounted for by the fact that some of the small schools may only have had one full-time member of staff. Almost half of the departments held meetings 'As required' and at irregular intervals, but this does not reveal a great deal of information, other than that many departments do not meet on a regular basis to discuss curriculum issues. No additional information was requested to clarify this question and further details are necessary.

Timing of meetings

It was apparent from the response to Question 14 that the majority of schools 83 per cent did not cater for departmental meetings in timetabled time. When meetings were held, they had to be conducted before or after the school day, at lunch times or during the vacation. The results of the previous section indicated irregular meetings for the majority of schools which could well be linked to this factor. However, approximately 17 per cent did plan for regular meetings to take place during the working day and half of these also met outside time-tabled time. Five schools (under 1 per cent) indicated that they did not meet at all.

Format of meetings

Three-quarters of the departments do not have meetings with a formal agenda and they obviously prefer alternative methods of conducting their business. A substantial number (41 per cent) ran the department meetings with a few guidelines, but the most common method (54 per cent) was through informal discussion. A combination of these styles was used in some instances. With a small number of staff who work closely together during the normal routine of the day, the staff may not feel a formal agenda to be appropriate. However, a formal agenda with the implied record of the decisions made, was being used in approximately a quarter of the schools.

The responses to the three questions in this section showed that nearly half the departments did not meet regularly, and that when they did meet, it was mostly in their own time and in an informal manner. In most physical education departments, all staff are involved in extra-curricular activities and this makes attendance at meetings a problem. The general impression tended to confirm an earlier suggestion that the planning is not as systematic as it might be.

Influencing factors

In this section, the teachers were asked to indicate on a five point scale which ranged from 'Very important' to 'Not important at all', the importance they attached to a list of 23 factors which may have influenced their planning of the physical education curriculum. They were asked to place a tick in the appropriate space opposite each item. In recording the responses, a score of 5 was given to 'Very important' and 1 to 'Not important at all', but the numerical score was not written on the questionnaire. *Table 26* shows the percentage of respondents who recorded 'important' or 'very important' and the ranking for each item.

Table 26. Influencing factors: teachers' assessment of importance

Item	Influencing Factor	% rating important or very important	Rank
1	Interests & abilities of PE staff	91.1	6
2	Help offered by non-P.E. staff	72.6	12
3	Use of external qualified coaches	31.9	22
4	Adequate facilities	98.2	1
5	Adequate financial provision	89.3	8
6	Use of local community facilities	56.7	16
7	Timetable allocation	96.5	2
8	Traditions of school	55.5	17
9	Attitude of school staff to PE	48.2	20
10	Ability to offer choice at some stage	89.4	7
11	Sport in local area	63.5	15
12	Democratic discussion with PE staff	85.8	9
13	Cultural values	48.9	19
14	Aims of physical education	95.4	3
15	Needs of society	65.8	14
16	Suggestions by PE advisers	45.8	21
17	Needs of other school subjects	31.1	23
18	Personal needs of child	92.8	5
19	Range of abilities within classes	69.9	13
20	Interests of children	74.0	11
21	Age of children	84.8	10
22	Assessment procedures	52.3	18
23	Logical progression	94.6	4

The six items considered to be the most important influencing factors are ranked in *Table 27*.

Table 27. Highest ranked influencing factors

Item	Influencing factor	Rank
4	Adequate facilities	1
7	Timetable allocation	2
14	Aims of physical education	3
23	Logical progression	4
18	Personal needs of the child	5
1	Interests & abilities of PE staff	6

At the other end of the scale, six items considered to be the least important influencing factors are ranked in *Table 28*.

Table 28. Lowest ranked influencing factors

Item	Influencing factor	Rank
22	Assessment procedures	18
13	Cultural values	19
9	Attitude of school staff to PE	20
16	Suggestions by PE advisers	21
3	Use of external qualified coaches	22
17	Needs of other school subjects	23

Greatest importance was attached to four main areas. The first related to organization within the school and incorporated the use of facilities, timetable allocation and adequate financial provision. The second was subject orientated and the aims of the subject figured prominently. The importance of logical progression and the ability to offer choice at some stage were also included in this grouping. Closely related to the subject was the third area which was concerned with the personal needs of the children. The fourth area focussed on the interests and abilities of the staff within the department and stressed the importance of democratic discussion with colleagues. Each of these items was considered to be important or very important by 85 per cent or more of the sample.

Although some items are ranked low, it would be wrong to assume they are unimportant in all schools. For example, the use of external qualified coaches was considered to be very important in a few schools, but institutions which did not have the resources or opportunity to employ coaches would obviously consider it to be less important. Thus different items will have different degrees of importance according to the individual needs of the school.

A factor analysis was undertaken based on the intercorrelations between the teachers' ratings of the twenty-three items. Seven factors were produced and showed which items in the list were scored in a similar way and how they clustered together. The factors listed in *Table 29* were named after an inspection

Table 29. Influencing factors: major factors

Factor	Items
1 School climate	2,5,8,9,17,20
2 Subject procedures	16,17,22,23
3 Community resources	1,2,3,6
4 School resources	4,5,7,21,23
5 Societal values	11,13,14,15,17
6 Democratic atmosphere	10,12,13,14
7 Children's abilities & interests	19,20

of the relevant items. The factors named above have the items making the biggest contribution listed alongside. (For details see Appendix D.)

The largest factor, *school climate,* accounted for nearly 20 per cent of the variance and emphasized the importance of the school staff to physical education, the traditions of the school and the positive help that was offered by non-physical education staff to the development of the subject. The second factor, *subject procedures,* was related to the progression and assessment procedures in physical education. The third factor, *community resources,* referred to the use made of external qualified coaches and local community facilities, as well as to help offered within the school. Factor four referred to *school resources* and takes in items related to adequacy of facilities, financial provision and timetable allocation. The fifth factor, *societal values,* was concerned with the needs of society and also embraced the cultural and social factors in the community. Factor six, *democratic atmosphere,* related democratic discussion in the department to the opportunity to offer choice in the programme at some stage. The final factor linked together *children's abilities and interests.*

Analysis of variance

All seven factors were subjected to a one-way analysis of variance with seven main variables into which the sample data was divided (Region, Head of department, Sex of teacher, Age range, Type, Size and Sex of school), to test whether the means of the sub-samples were significantly different from each other.

A number of statistically significant differences were recorded against each of the seven influencing factors. School climate was given a statistically significant higher score by older teachers and by grammar schools. Additionally, schools under 1,000 pupils attached greater importance to this factor than schools with a larger population. One tentative interpretation of these differences might be that older teachers are more sensitive to the attitudes of their colleagues towards physical education and this may be especially true in grammar schools. Schools under 1,000 pupils may also be a closer knit community than some of the larger institutions and this might lead to more integration between the physical education department and other staff.

The only difference recorded in the second factor, subject procedures, was that females who were also heads of department in girls' schools scored significantly higher than their male colleagues. It appears that these teachers are greatly influenced by the logical development of the subject and also place more value on the suggestions of the advisory staff.

A number of statistically significant differences were apparent in the community resources factor. The factor was considered to be less important in larger institutions of more than 1,000 pupils, in single sex schools and in comprehensive schools. Possibly, larger schools with a mixed staff may have more human and physical resources available to them and do not need to rely on the local community resources. The exception to this was that all grammar schools scored the factor high. There were also regional differences with the South-East attaching more and the Midlands less importance than the other four regions.

Two statistically significant differences were apparent for school resources. The largest group of schools (over 1,500 pupils) considered the factor to be important and this may have been because large schools consider the provision of adequate facilities and finance to be essential when there are large numbers of pupils to cater for. In addition, heads of department in boys' schools scored this factor significantly lower than the other departmental heads, but the reasons for this are not apparent at this stage.

Societal values revealed no significant differences apart from older teachers (over 40 years) who considered this factor to be of greater importance than younger teachers (under 40 years) and the trend indicated a progressive increase in the importance of this factor as the teachers became older. This would suggest that teachers develop their work in a wider perspective as they became older, but this is a tentative interpretation.

The importance of a democratic atmosphere for both staff and pupils was most marked for the over 40 years age group. The smallest sized schools (under 500 pupils) scored low on this factor which may not reflect less importance, but simply the fact that there were fewer staff involved and therefore less need for democratic discussion and also possibly less opportunity to offer choice to the pupils.

Children's abilities and interests were considered to be more important by heads of girls' departments and female teachers. It also appeared that great heed was paid to this factor in girls' schools. A regional difference was apparent with the Midlands attaching less, and Wales more, importance than the other four regions. Apart from these, no other significant differences were revealed.

The overall impression was that there were a number of statistically significant differences, but no consistent pattern was revealed. The interpretations that have been made are speculative and some of the differences, for example regional variations, could only be interpreted by further investigation.

It is important to record that the majority of the analyses indicated no significant differences between the seven main sample variables and the seven influencing factors.

Discussion of major factors

1 The first factor referred to the importance of the school climate. The attitude of the school staff to physical education had a high loading on this factor, and the support and help offered by male academic staff as opposed to female staff, was statistically significant ($p<.01$) and was greatly appreciated. It is essential that the subject receives the same status as other subjects on the curriculum and this can best be done in a supportive environment which emanates from the Headteacher and senior staff. The building up of traditions and the setting of standards for pupils can be attained by the head of department and his staff insisting on a professional approach to teaching. This is one way of establishing respect for the subject in the school and ensuring the contribution physical education makes to the education of children is recognized by all staff.

2 The value of establishing subject procedures has been stressed at various times during the study and this was the name given to the second factor. The need for logical progression in the work was specially emphasized and this should relate to all aspects of teaching, from the common core in the first year to the optional activities in senior forms. There is no justification in giving more thought and preparation to the common core and less to the options, as all aspects of work are equally important and the planning should reflect this. Another contributory item to this factor was assessment procedures. The measurement of progress in the overt areas of the subject, for example, motor skills, is quite well documented. Many of the governing bodies of sport provide hierarchical award schemes which are frequently used in schools. This contrasts with the more covert areas such as moral and social development, where the assessment procedures are not so clear cut and are based on personal interpretations. Much of the recording of an individual's progress in physical education throughout the school is done in a haphazard manner and there is a requirement for simple yet systematic methods of recording which are not too time consuming.

3 It was clear that teachers seized upon the use of community resources and facilities when it was practical to do so. This not only applied to physical resources that may have been available in the local area, such as sports centres and swimming pools, but also to the use of personnel outside the physical education department who had expertise in a particular activity. The help given by male colleagues in particular, was essential to the running of a thriving extra-curricular activities programme. It was apparent that larger schools with a mixed staff attached a lower level of importance to community resources than other types of school. This may have been due to the fact that larger institutions would probably have more resources available. However, if

additional facilities are available in the local community, they can have a substantial influence on the total programme. Care needs to be taken to ensure excessive time is not spent in travelling, but provided facilities are nearby and the timetable can be blocked, the community resources can enhance the range of activities offered in the curriculum.

4 The fourth factor 'school resources' embraced the provision of suitable facilities to conduct the work of the department, adequate finance to purchase equipment for a wide range of activities and an appropriate timetable allocation. All these were considered essential to run a department efficiently and were particularly emphasized in the largest schools and by heads of department in boys' schools. There is no doubt that the place of physical education in the curriculum is determined by the Headteacher and senior staff, and indicates the need for a strong case to be made for the subject to Headteachers and faculty meetings. (The importance of the Headteachers' influence had also emerged in the first factor). The necessity for clear documentation, rational argument and high standards of work is again emphasized in influencing the allocation of resources within a school.

5 The fifth factor, named societal values, placed the subject in a much wider context. A broad base was apparent from the loadings on the needs of society and cultural values. These items were also linked to the aims of the subject and sport in the local area, and these may in turn have been related to the participation of pupils in leisure and recreation once they had left school. With the increasing emphasis on accountability in education, the relationship of physical education to society will be an important consideration.

6 The importance of a democratic atmosphere within the physical education department has been evident on more than one occasion. It can lead to a full contribution from all staff and there was support for this from the analysis. Heads of department, especially those over 40 years, appeared to welcome contributions from their colleagues about the planning of the curriculum and this form of consultation should be encouraged. The democratic atmosphere not only referred to the staff, but also to the children in the form of offering some choice within the programme at some stage. Occasionally, the programme can be strongly influenced by the declared interests of the children, particularly in the presentation of the optional activities programmes.

7 No curriculum can be effective without taking the abilities and interests of the children into consideration. They are central to the educational process. Ability levels should influence the planning of work if suitable learning experiences are to be offered to all children. This applies to the very good where excellence should be pursued, and also to the less able who should achieve success appropriate to their level of ability. The inter-relationship of skill levels, attitudes and understanding can only be fully achieved if appropriate experiences are offered initially. As the pupils enter the senior school, almost all departments incorporate an optional activities programme. Occasionally, this offers a completely free choice, but more often a guided choice. This is one of the ways in which individual interests can be catered for. It

appeared that greater heed was paid to this factor by female teachers, which may suggest that they adopt a more 'child-centred' approach to their teaching than their males colleagues.

Planning of boys' and girls' programmes

Where the school population was mixed, the teachers were asked if the male and female staff planned the boys' and girls' programmes separately or together. There was an almost equal division of response by the sample (N=434). Thus half the teachers planned with all their colleagues and the other half planned independently. There was, however, a significant difference (p.<.01) which indicated that male teachers were more likely to plan the programmes together than their female colleagues. Obviously there must be collaboration about the use of such physical resources as equipment and facilities, but it is surprising that there is not a greater degree of integration, particularly in the optional activity programme in the senior forms.

Common core

Question 18 sought to establish the frequency of a common core of activities in physical education which all the children of any one year group must follow. Responses indicated that 92 per cent of the schools did operate a system whereby all children followed the same programme of activities at some stage. How this varied from year to year is shown in *Table 30.*

Table 30. Common core activities: Years 1–6

Common core activities	% Yes	% No
Year 1	98	2
Year 2	97	3
Year 3	91	9
Year 4	52	48
Year 5	22	78
Year 6	5	95

The common core of activity decreased the longer the child was in school, but there was little change during the first three years. Inevitably linked to this was an increase in the amount of choice offered to the pupils. No marked change was apparent until the end of Year 3.

Optional activities

There was an element of choice in all years, but it was most marked in Years 4,

5 and 6. In the final year it amounted to 95 per cent of the time and totally dominated the curriculum. Where this element of choice does exist, there are often problems in relation to adequate supervision and teaching, especially when groups are small. Question 19 was structured to ascertain the degree of instruction pupils received during optional activities. It is heartening to record that over 90 per cent were nearly always under instruction, but this left 9 per cent who were only occasionally or rarely under instruction.

In a physical education context, it is acceptable for children to be allowed to work on their own, provided that the normal safety rules are being observed. However, it is essential that they are not left to practise on their own for too long, have an understanding of the activity and a clear indication what they should be doing. It is when children are given equipment and told to engage in the activity, with little or no guidance and instruction, that serious questions arise about its educational value.

A statistical analysis revealed no significant differences between region, age range, type, size and sex of school and the degree of instruction received during the optional activities programme. The sex of the teacher did however reveal significant differences and there was a greater likelihood that the children would be under instruction if the teacher was female and head of girls' physical education. This may be linked to the earlier suggestion that female teachers give greater emphasis to the abilities and interests of children in their planning.

Method of planning

This section was concerned with some of the ways in which teachers set about planning their physical education programmes. In particular, the respondents were asked if an official written physical education syllabus was in existence in the school, to which 91 per cent gave a positive answer. This represented a high return and indicated that most schools had written documentation available. The remaining 9 per cent gave a negative reply.

Planning the syllabus

Table 31 summarizes the type of sources teachers refer to when planning a syllabus.

Nearly two-thirds of the sample referred to books and half to articles in their planning. There were no details concerning the number or type of references used but over one-third did not make use of this source in their preparation. Forty-four per cent took external advice of some kind and this particular item could have been interpreted by the head of department as external to himself, the department or the school.

The average length of teaching for the sample was 12 years. When one

Table 31. Syllabus planning: sources of reference

Reference	% Yes	% No
Refer to books	66	34
Refer to articles	50	50
Take external advice	44	56
Refer to college course	62	38
Refer to other PE syllabuses	62	38
Obtain ideas from in-service courses	61	39
Use own ideas	96	4
Other	4	96

considers the changes that have taken place in education during the last two decades, it is surprising that 62 per cent are still referring to their college course.

There was an indication from the interviews with teachers which had taken place during the initial stages of the study, that few of them had seen any physical education syllabuses other than their own. However, in this sample, 62 per cent stated they had referred to other syllabuses which indicated a wide range of consultation. It was also heartening to record that 61 per cent had obtained ideas from in-service courses which tended to confirm the usefulness of such courses and the commitment of physical educationists in attending them. No two schools are identical and a great number of individual ideas and initiatives have to be developed to devise a dynamic syllabus which will work in particular circumstances. The fact that 96 per cent 'used their own ideas' leant support to the innovatory nature of much of the planning.

Opportunity was available for the teachers to make additional comments and 22 schools suggested alternative considerations, the most common being inter-departmental discussion. These took the form of pure verbal interchange as well as teachers responsible for specialist areas submitting written documents for comment. Four teachers had welcomed the opportunity to visit other schools and talk to the teachers and advisers about syllabus planning. The local environment, social and physical, and its influence on planning was also mentioned. One school had carried out a pupil survey ascertaining likes and dislikes in physical activity and used the results as a guide to planning.

Revision of syllabus

Once a syllabus has been written, rapid educational change can soon make it obsolete. Syllabus revision appeared to have taken place quite recently in most cases, as 52 per cent had carried out a revision during the last academic year and a further 37 per cent during the last 2–3 years. However, 5 per cent had not been revised for 5 years or more and nearly half of this last group had not been revised at all.

Revision can be carried out by a variety of people and Question 23 asked which person or persons were involved. In the majority of instances, either the head of department on his own (55 per cent) or the full department (67 per cent) took part in the revision. In 12 per cent of the sample, only a section of the department took part, presumably those specialist members of staff who were solely concerned with that particular aspect of the curriculum. Additional advice sometimes came from external advisers (11 per cent) who could have been external to the department such as the Headteacher, or external to the school such as the local advisory staff.

The overall impression from the above data was one of schools having a written syllabus available which was under frequent review. It had been formulated in the school and many sources had been referred to in the planning stages. These results would appear to be in contrast to the syllabus planning ideas obtained in the original interviews. The questionnaire did not allow for more detailed probing and it would have been interesting to have elicited a more detailed analysis of what exactly constituted a syllabus. There may well be differences of opinion concerning the meaning of terms such as syllabus, schemes of work and departmental policy statements, and these need to be clarified in order that meaningful comparisons can be made.

Time analysis of subjects

It is possible to analyze the number of hours devoted to each physical education activity and this is usually referred to as a 'time analysis'. In order to ascertain the balance in a programme this type of analysis can be helpful. The majority of teachers (61 per cent) did conduct such an exercise but there were quite a substantial number (39 per cent) who either did not consider this to be worthwhile or who had not thought of doing it. Two statistically significant differences were revealed. These indicated that there was less likelihood that a time analysis had been carried out in the North and Midlands area ($p<.01$) as well as in grammar schools ($p<.05$). One possible explanation for the school difference might be that the programme in grammar schools has been functioning for a number of years with comparatively fewer upheavals in school organization than has occurred in other types of secondary schools. Thus there would be less likelihood of the necessity for a time analysis to be carried out. However, this interpretation is very tentative. An explanation of the regional differences is difficult without further information.

Depth of planning

Question 25 asked if departments planned for links between the different activities. Ninety per cent reported positively and it appeared there was a conscious effort by the vast majority to make links between the differing subject content in physical education.

The next question asked if more thought was given to the planning of progressions for the 'common core' of work than for the optional activities. The responses are summarized in *Table 32*.

Table 32. Depth of planning for common core and optional activities

Depth of planning for common core as against optional activities.	%
Much more	51
Slightly more	27
Same	20
Slightly less	1
Much less	1

It was apparent that over three-quarters of the teachers gave more thought and preparation to the common core of work, whereas only 2 per cent gave more thought to the planning of the optional activities. This lends weight to the suggestion that teachers plan their common core work in some depth and that optional activity programmes are not planned so diligently.

Purpose of planning

The first question in this section stated that aims and objectives, content, method and evaluation were generally regarded as four important factors in curriculum planning. Respondents were asked to judge the proportion of their syllabus which was associated with these areas by allocating some part of 100 per cent to each (total must equal 100). In order to obtain a qualitative judgement, the proportion allocated was to be guided by the emphasis given to the statements rather than the number of words written.

The purposes of this question were twofold. One was to determine the importance that heads of department attached to these four main aspects of planning and the other was to make a comparison with the earlier analysis of the written syllabuses that had been carried out by independent judges. The results of the present survey are set out in *Table 33*.

Table 33. Percentages allocated to four aspects of planning

Aspect of planning	%	S.D.	Range
Aims & objectives	25	9.6	0–100
Content	36	12.9	0–100
Teaching method	24	8.9	0–60
Evaluation	15	7.2	0–30

Greatest emphasis was placed on the content of the syllabus (36 per cent). Aims and objectives and teaching method both recorded approximately 25 per cent and evaluation 15 per cent. The standard deviations indicated less variance for the importance attached to the aspect of evaluation than for the other three areas. Whilst the central measures were clear, there was a considerable range of scores outside these. For aims and objectives and content, scores were recorded at both ends of the scale *ie.* 0 per cent and 100 per cent. This revealed a complete spectrum of opinion from those who attached no importance to these factors, to those who considered them to be the totality of planning. For teaching method the range was 0 per cent to 60 per cent and for the evaluation 0 per cent to 30 per cent. For these two factors, the range is reducing. However it still indicates a wide range of opinion. Whilst general trends can be identified there were many individual variations.

A comparison with the earlier analysis undertaken by independent judges in Chapter 4, Analysis 1 produced the following data (*Table 34*).

Table 34. Comparison of percentages allocated by judges and teachers (self-rating) to four aspects of planning.

	Aims & Objectives %	Content %	Method %	Evaluation %
Independent judges	15	61	19	5
Teachers – (Self-rating)	25	36	24	15

An inspection of the above table revealed obvious differences in emphasis, but it is important to note the two groups were not analyzing the same syllabuses. Whilst content received the highest proportion from both groups, the independent judges awarded a much higher percentage in this area. The judges gave less emphasis than the teachers to aims and objectives, method and evaluation. The results supported the notion that content received the most and evaluation the least emphasis in planning. However, the self-rating by teachers indicated a much more even distribution between the four components. The implication here is that the emphasis teachers put upon their own written syllabuses may be interpreted differently by other people. Again the need for clarity and precision is highlighted. Discussion of the written syllabus within the department, with senior colleagues and advisers, and open presentation at in-service courses may help to alleviate any misconceptions.

One-way analysis of variance and chi-square calculations of the seven main variables (Region, Head of Department, Sex, Age range, Type, Size, Sex of school) with aims and objectives, content, method and evaluation revealed few statistically significant differences. Region, age range and type of school produced no significant differences for any of the four curriculum components under scrutiny. Additionally, none of the variables were significantly different in the emphasis they placed on aims and objectives. Only one variable, size of school, showed a significant difference with content and indicated that small schools were more likely to attach less importance to this aspect of planning. This may be simply because of the fewer staff involved. There were also indications that the heads of girls' physical education and female teachers in girls' schools were less likely to apportion the same importance to teaching method as their male colleagues in boys' or mixed schools. All these findings were at the 5 per cent or 1 per cent level of statistical significance. Six of the seven variables showed no difference in their rating of evaluation in planning. The one exception was the size of school which suggested that small schools were more likely to attach greater importance to the evaluation component.

The overall results showed very little difference between the main variables and indicated a high degree of agreement between teachers and the proportion of their syllabus they associated with the four areas of curriculum planning.

Intention of the plan

In question 28, teachers were asked to rate fourteen purposes that the planning of the curriculum might have for them. As for the section on Influencing

Table 35. Purposes of planning: teachers' assessment of importance.

Item	Purpose	% rating important of very important	Rank
1	As a guide to the PE staff	95.0	1=
2	As a guide to the subject	85.9	7
3	As a way of suggesting teaching methods	57.0	12
4	As a consideration of children's needs whilst at school	93.9	3
5	As a consideration of children's needs once they have left school	89.0	6
6	To ensure efficient use of resources and facilities	93.8	4
7	To ensure continuity in teaching	95.0	1=
8	To state the aims of PE	74.0	10
9	As a guide to the children	29.0	14
10	To utilize staff expertise	84.2	8
11	To be consistent with school philosophy	51.2	13
12	To enable Head of Dept. to co-ordinate work	82.4	9
13	To provide suitable learning experiences	91.4	5
14	To ensure adequate evaluation	60.9	11

Factors, each purpose could be rated on a five-point scale which ranged fom 'Very important' to 'Not important at all'. The percentage of respondents who recorded 'important' or 'very important' and the ranking for each item is set out in *Table 35*.
The six items considered to have the most important purpose in the planning of the physical education curriculum are ranked in *Table 36*.

Table 36. Highest ranked purposes of planning

Item	Purpose of planning	Rank
1	As a guide to the PE staff	1=
7	To ensure continuity in teaching	1=
4	As a consideration of children's needs whilst at school	3
6	To ensure efficient use of resources and facilities	4
13	To provide suitable learning experiences	5
5	As a consideration of children's needs once they have left school	6

The most important rankings were to guide the physical education staff, provide a framework for the subject and ensure continuity in the teaching, as well as ensuring efficiency in the use of the resources and facilities. The value of providing suitable learning experiences for the children while at school and in preparation for their needs once they had left school also figured prominently. The utilization of the expertise of the staff and the co-ordination role carried out by heads of department both received a high rating of importance. However, even for items which were lowly ranked, there were still some schools who classed these items as 'very important'. This indicated that some items will have varying degrees of influence in different schools.

Table 37. Purposes of planning: major factors

Factor	Items
1. Co-ordination & continuity	6,7,8,11,12,13,14
2. Guidance for the children	3,9
3. Children's needs	4,5
4. Subject guide for staff	1,2,12

A factor analysis was undertaken based on the inter-correlations between the teachers' ratings of the fourteen items. Four factors were produced which described the main underlying structure of the items and the manner in which they clustered together. The factors listed in *Table 37* were named after an inspection of the relevant items. The factors listed above have the items making the biggest contribution listed alongside (For details, see Appendix D).

Factor one, *co-ordination and continuity*, was large and accounted for 24 per cent of the variance in purposes of planning in the curriculum. Seven items contributed to this factor and reflected efficiency in the department as well as in the organization of the subject. The second factor, *guidance for the children*, had a high loading on one item of the same name and was linked with teaching methods. The third factor was concerned with the needs of children whilst at school and once they had left school. The factor was named *children's needs*. The last factor, *subject guide for staff*, linked together items which described guidance for the subject as well as for the staff.

Analysis of variance

The four purposes of planning factors were subjected to a one-way analysis of variance with the seven main sample variables to test whether the means of the sub-samples were significantly different from each other.

The most important observation was that there were few statistically significant differences. The purposes of planning the physical education curriculum were remarkably consistent within the seven variables in the sample. In one of the factors, children's needs, no differences were revealed. The factor, guidance for children, showed no significant differences apart from single sex schools who scored this factor significantly lower than mixed schools. The factor, co-ordination and continuity, showed a significantly lower score for the head of boys' physical education, but apart from this there were no other differences. It is difficult to explain this, because there were also men who were heads of mixed departments and the difference cannot be attributed to a sex variable. The other factor, subject guide for staff, was found to be more important in larger schools which is not surprising as there would also be a larger number of staff involved in the teaching.

The over-riding interpretation was therefore one with few significant differences between regions, teachers and schools and the four main purposes of planning factors which had been identified in curriculum planning.

Discussion of major factors

1 The first factor was concerned with co-ordination in the department and continuity in teaching. An efficient head of department should be able to identify the objectives to be pursued and the teaching strategies to be followed, as well as making the best use of the resources available. These resources include the physical resources available such as gymnasia, sports hall and playing fields, as well as the efficient deployment of the human resources on the staff. Heads of department should try to ensure there is continuity in the subject planning both within and between each year. This can be done through

progressive planning of the syllabus. It seems there is greater continuity in the common core of work than in the optional activities programme. This trend was confirmed earlier in the questionnaire where over three-quarters gave more thought and preparation to the core programme. This should not be the case as all aspects of the curriculum should be planned and prepared with equal care and attention. There is no doubt that the co-ordinating role played by the departmental head is a major factor in the efficient running of a department.

2 The factor 'guidance for children' appeared and was named because of the high loading of one item of the same name. This was surprising because most teachers did not communicate the aims of physical education to the children they taught and when it did occur, it was usually done informally and unsystematically. There was, however, a greater tendency to outline shorter-term objectives especially in the more objective aspects, where it was easier to specify the skills and behaviours to be attained. On the other hand, if the aims of the subject are considered important enough to communicate to children, then suitable methods need to be identified to achieve this. Otherwise there will be misinterpretations and misconceptions about the subject. Clearly, further details about this factor are needed and more detailed examination is warranted.

3 The needs of children must inevitably receive consideration in any enlightened syllabus. This factor had permeated some of the earlier discussions and was confirmed as an important factor in the questionnaire. Children's needs were considered in the planning of the curriculum, as well as in the large number of extra-curricular activities, which were freely available to most children regardless of ability. The highest loading was recorded against children's needs once they had left school and indicated the importance attached to participation in leisure and recreative facilities. This was certainly consistent with the emphasis placed on the purposeful use of leisure time as an aim of physical education.

4 The purpose of any syllabus must inevitably incorporate guidance for the subject and staff who teach it. These two items had moderate loadings on the factor 'subject guide for staff'. The emergence of this factor stresses the need for efficient planning and well presented syllabuses in physical education. Such documentation not only acts as a permanent record of the work of the department, but also gives a sense of direction and purpose for the staff.

Communication

Where there is more than one person in a department, any plan that exists for the teaching of physical education has to be communicated effectively to colleagues. This section of the questionnaire attempted to ascertain the extent of the communication pattern.

Communication with physical education colleagues

Question 29 suggested four ways in which the curriculum plan could be communicated to colleagues in the physical education department. The results are set out in *Table 38.*

Table 38. Methods of communication: PE staff

Communication with PE staff	% Yes	% No
Entire written syllabus	65	35
Parts of written syllabus	16	84
Regular verbal guidelines	61	39
Verbal guidelines at the start of the term	38	62

Heads of department communicated with their staff in a variety of ways, the most common of which were through the complete written syllabus and regular verbal guidelines. With 81 per cent communicating through the written word, this still left a substantial number of departments who did not communicate their curriculum plan through the syllabus. The day to day contact of staff in physical education departments would be conducive to verbal exchanges and the results of the above table tend to confirm this. Nevertheless, it is surprising that approximately one-third of the sample did not distribute a copy of the complete syllabus to their colleagues in the department.

Communication with non-physical education staff

Quite a different pattern emerged for communicating the plan to the non-physical education staff *ie.* colleagues in other departments whose teaching was predominantly in another subject but who taught a few periods of physical education.

The findings are summarized in *Table 39.*

Table 39. Methods of communication: non-PE staff

Communication with non-PE staff	% Yes	% No
Entire written syllabus	26	74
Parts of written syllabus	23	77
Regular verbal guidelines	56	44
Verbal guidelines at the start of the term	33	67

Almost half received a copy of the entire written syllabus or a relevant part of it. Regular verbal guidelines were the most common method of communication and verbal exchange was used much more frequently than the written word. Staff who make a small contribution to the teaching of physical education are often quite able performers in the activity. However, this does not imply that they are necessarily good teachers. They should be given advice about content and progression within the activity and many might also welcome practical suggestions about teaching.

Supervision of courses

Where heads of department were responsible for the planning of a course which was carried out by someone else, they were almost equally divided between checking frequently (46 per cent) and making infrequent checks (52 per cent). The remaining 2 per cent made no checks at all. This indicates a firm commitment by departmental heads to ensure that courses are taught effectively. Although teachers have a great deal of autonomy in the manner in which they teach, they must conform to an overall plan. Whether the checks were made by attending lessons, consulting records or through discussion was not ascertained.

Specifying teaching style

The extent to which a particular teaching style was specified for the different activities in physical education was probed in question 32. A small group (15 per cent) specified 'fairly often' and an even smaller group (2 per cent) 'always'. The majority (67 per cent) used the categories 'sometimes' or 'rarely', but 16 per cent clearly 'never' specified the teaching style that should be adopted by a colleague in their department. Clearly, heads of department do not always specify teaching styles, but there was greater likelihood ($p<.01$) that it would be done in comprehensive and secondary modern/high schools than in grammar schools. However, age and sex differences were not found to be statistically significant in the present sample. An observation might indicate that it is more likely that suggestions will be made about the advisability of using a particular style in certain circumstances. For example, directed teaching is often recommended when the safety of the pupils is involved. In the main, teachers appear to have a great deal of autonomy about the style of teaching they adopt and there is little imposition from heads of department.

Communicating aims and objectives

Questions 33 and 34 attempted to ascertain the extent to which teachers communicated to children the long-term aims of physical education and the short-term objectives of a course. *Table 40* shows the distribution of their replies.

Table 40. Communication of long-term aims and short-term objectives

Communication method	Long-term aims %	Short-term objectives %
Almost always	15	38
Usually	33	44
Occasionally	41	14
Rarely	9	3
Never	2	1

There was a greater inclination for teachers to communicate the short-term objectives of a course than the long-term aims of the subject. This could have been due to the more tangible nature of objectives and the fact that they were more likely to be realized in the foreseeable future by the children. However, a chi-square of the following sub-sections of the sample (Region, Head of department, Sex, Age range, and Type of School) with the communication of long-term and short-term objectives revealed no statistically significant differences. This suggested that the extent to which teachers communicated aims and objectives to children did not differ. The literature review had suggested there might be age and sex variables, but this was not confirmed in this analysis.

The above table lends support to the notion that many teachers do not communicate aims and objectives to the children and this can only result in haphazard learning about the purposes of physical education.

Evaluation

The final section of the questionnaire was concerned with the different methods used to judge the success of the physical education programme and the role played by evaluation in the curriculum process.

Pupils' progress

Most school subjects have a clearly defined examination system and method for recording results. The situation is not the same in physical education and question 35 asked the teachers to indicate the methods they used to record pupils' progress against a prepared list, with the opportunity to make their own observations. The responses are tabulated in *Table 41*.

Table 41. Methods of recording pupils' progress

Recording pupils' progress	% Yes	% No
Termly report	66	34
Annual report	45	55
Department book	31	69
Numerical grades	25	75
Literal grades	33	67
Card-index filing system	16	84
Representative honours	65	35
Other	6	94

The school report was an obvious method of recording progress and 66 per cent sent their comments out termly and 45 per cent annually. The sum of these two exceeds 100 per cent which suggested a biannual report in some cases. A quarter used numerical grades and a third literal grades to record progress with the remainder using alternative methods. Departmental records were kept by means of a department book (31 per cent) or a card-index filing system (16 per cent). This left slightly more than half who did not use either of these two methods to keep a systematic record of pupils' progress in the department. Representative honours figured prominently in the recording procedure for 65 per cent of the schools.

Other methods mentioned included the use of House standards, school colours and the importance staff attached to pupils' ability, attitude and effort in all the courses offered. Objective tests were referred to and these were often linked to the national award schemes in a number of physical activities. In one school, an elaborate system of progressive skills testing had been devized at the request of the pupils. Single instances of subject prizes and school news letters were also mentioned.

Question 36 asked the teachers to indicate whether or not they considered ability, effort and physical fitness when recording pupils' progress. The results are set out in *Table 42*.

Table 42. Recording pupils' progress in ability, effort and physical fitness.

Recording pupils' progress	% Yes	% No
Ability	92	8
Effort	99	1
Physical fitness	42	58

Almost without exception, 99 per cent of the sample considered the effort pupils put into their work to be an essential factor in recording progress. Similarly, a very high proportion (92 per cent) regarded the pupils' ability levels as important. Standards of physical fitness were used less frequently by

42 per cent. From this last group there were no significant differences from the sub-sections of the sample.

School reports were the most common method used to convey to the parents the progress being made by their child in physical education. This was done by means of written comments and numerical or literal grades. Teachers responded to the suggestion that the space provided in the school report was unlimited (10 per cent), restricted but adequate (70 per cent) and restricted and inadequate (20 per cent). It appeared that one-fifth were dissatisfied with the format of the report in their school. Presumably the format did not allow teachers to make a full profile of children's development in physical education. There is some cause for concern here because many schools are not keeping departmental records and are relying on the accumulated evidence from school reports. If the system adopted in the school is inadequate, then the subsequent pupil profile will also be inadequate.

Evaluating original aims

Question 38 asked if the heads of department systematically attempted to evaluate their original aims of physical education. The responses showed that 44 per cent made such an evaluation 'often' or 'a great deal'. The most frequent response (47 per cent) was only 'occasionally', and for 9 per cent the reply was 'rarely' or 'never'.

Evaluation and future planning

Teachers were asked to respond to five categories regarding the effect evaluation had in influencing the planning of future courses. *Table 43* summarizes the data.

Table 43. Evaluation and future planning

Evaluation and future planning	%
Always	26
Fairly often	37
Sometimes	33
Rarely	3
Never	1

In an analysis of the sub-sections of the sample, one significant difference ($p<.05$) was revealed which suggested that female teachers were more likely to use evaluation procedures in the above contexts than their male colleagues. This reasons for this are not apparent, but further investigation of this difference is warranted.

An investigation of the evaluation of the original aims of the subject and their relationship to the part played by evaluation in influencing future planning produced the following information (Table 44).

Table 44. Relationship between the evaluation of original aims and future planning.

		Influencing future planning				
		Always %	Fairly often %	Sometimes %	Rarely %	Never %
Evaluating original aims	A great deal	6	1	0	0	0
	Often	13	17	6	0	0
	Occasionally	6	18	23	1	0
	Rarely	1	1	4	2	0
	Never	0	0	0	0	1

In the first two categories for each variable, a total of 37 per cent was recorded which indicated the percentage of the sample using evaluation to look back to their original aims as well as looking forward to future planning. The most common cell in the table 'occasionally' evaluated aims and 'sometimes' used evaluation for planning future courses. Only 3 per cent 'rarely' or 'never' used evaluation for these purposes. The results indicated a greater likelihood that the evaluation procedures would be orientated towards the future and have a bigger influence on the construction of new courses. There was less inclination for teachers to look back and make a systematic evaluation about achieving their aims of physical education.

The integral part curriculum theorists suggest evaluation plays in the curriculum process is not supported by the above data, as many teachers do not incorporate evaluative procedures into their curriculum planning to any great extent.

Evaluation of curriculum planning

The final question asked teachers to consider some of the methods that are used to judge the success of their curriculum planning. Fifteen methods were listed and responses were rated on a five-point scale which ranged from 'very important' to 'not important at all'. The percentage of respondents who recorded 'important' or 'very important' and the ranking for each item is set out in *Table 45*.

The six items considered to be most used in judging the success of courses are ranked in *Table 46*.

Table 45. Methods of evaluation: teachers' assessment of importance

Item	Method	% rating important or very important	Rank
1	Maintaining school traditions	56.4	13
2	Participation in post school recreation	93.7	5
3	Objective measurement	55.3	14
4	Subjective opinion	58.1	11
5	Enjoyment	98.2	2
6	Development of good attitudes	99.6	1
7	Working atmosphere	95.2	3
8	Skill levels	94.3	4
9	Success in external competition	57.4	12
10	Fitness levels	79.0	8
11	Extra-curricular participation	90.7	6
12	Social competence	82.1	7
13	Aesthetic appreciation	63.6	9
14	Parental interest	59.5	10
15	Other teachers' opinions	37.9	15

Table 46. Highest ranked methods of evaluation

Item	Method	Rank
6	Development of good attitudes	1
5	Enjoyment	2
7	Working atmosphere	3
8	Skill levels	4
2	Participation in post school recreation	5
11	Extra-curricular participation	6

The items ranked in the above table suggested the heads of department regarded the affective areas of attitude and enjoyment, the development of skill in a good working atmosphere and participation in extra-curricular and post school recreation to be the most important methods by which they judged the success of their planning. Two other high scoring variables not in the above table, referred to social competence and the attainment of standards of physical fitness.

Opportunity was given to suggest other evaluation methods and several teachers did respond. The majority referred to the importance of voluntary participation by children at all levels of ability as well as developing competence in a few activities. Cognitive aspects such as knowledge and understanding of the physical activities, with special reference to fitness, were also mentioned.

Table 47. Methods of evaluation: major factors

Factor	Items
1. Aesthetic and social appreciation	12,13,14
2. Leisure participation	2,5,6,11,12,14
3. Standards	1,9,14,15
4. Climate	6,7
5. Motor development	3,8,10

A factor analysis based on the intercorrelations between the teachers' scores on fifteen items was undertaken. Five factors were produced which described the main underlying structure of the items and the manner in which they clustered together. *Table 47* describes and lists five factors, together with the main items which contribute to them (For details see Appendix D).

The first factor, *aesthetic and social appreciation*, accounted for 21 per cent of the variance and emphasized aesthetic appreciation, social competence and parental interest. Factor two, *leisure participation*, related to the emphasis on participation in post school recreation and extra-curricular activity. Factor three, *standards*, was concerned with school traditions, success in competition and other teachers' opinions. The fourth factor covered the development of good attitudes and the working atmosphere surrounding the subject and was named *climate*. The last factor emphasized *motor development* through skill and fitness levels.

Analysis of variance

Each of the five evaluation factors was subjected to a one-way analysis of variance with the seven main variables into which the sample data was divided to test whether the means of the sub-samples were significantly different from each other.

Female teachers scored significantly higher than male teachers on the two factors of aesthetic and social appreciation, and climate. It would be reasonable to expect female teachers to attach greater importance to aesthetic appreciation and a separate analysis of this particular item revealed this to be the case. The indication that they regard the working climate to be more important than their male colleagues is unexpected. The factor entitled standards, assumed a higher score as teachers became older, as well as in grammar schools. This may be due to the development of the personal standards of teachers, and the maintaining of the traditions of external competition in the older grammar schools. Significantly higher scores for motor development were recorded in schools with 1,000 to 1,500 pupils, in contrast to lower scores in small schools under 500 pupils and very large schools of over 1,500 pupils. These differences cannot be explained without further information.

For every other analysis, no significant differences were revealed, which indicated a high level of consistency in the methods of evaluation used by teachers in the differing schools in the regions.

Discussion of major factors

1 The first factor, named aesthetic and social appreciation, derived its name from two major loading items entitled aesthetic appreciation and social competence. The socializing effects of physical education is an important aim, but the aesthetic component is less generally recognized. One significant difference ($p<.01$) was that female teachers considered this factor to be more important than their male colleagues and this applied particularly to the aesthetic aspect. The content of the subject offered in girls' physical education will invariably include dance and educational gymnastics which lend themselves more readily to this kind of subjective evaluation, whereas the boys' programmes usually offers educational gymnastics in the first two years, but rarely includes dance. Thus there were a number of variations concerning the importance of this factor.

2 Participation in leisure activities outside the timetabled curriculum was the next factor in evaluating courses. This referred to extra-curricular activities as well as post-school recreation. Occasionally, the impression was given that the clubs were elitist and more important than the actual curriculum work carried out during the school day. This was particularly true in the sphere of competitive games where success appeared to be the sole criterion for judging the efficiency of the physical education department. A more balanced view regards them as offering additional opportunity to develop skill and achieve excellence. The majority of extra-curricular activities should be open to all children with some ability and keenness being the main attributes for joining. It is important to attract the children with high levels of ability and the teaching and coaching should cater for the differing abilities. As well as the extra participation at school, the degree of involvement in physical activity by pupils once they had left school is also an important long-term measure of the success of the subject. This was one of the main aims for men and women teachers and was regarded by 94 per cent of the sample as an important method of evaluation. Minor loadings on social competence, development of good attitudes and enjoyment gave some indication of the general working atmosphere to be aimed for in this aspect of physical education.

3 Standards set within any school or department are an indication of the kinds of criteria that have to be met by the staff responsible for that subject. Success in external competition had an influence on the naming of this factor, and for this particular item, a statistical difference ($p<.05$) was revealed which

indicated that the head of a girls' physical education department was more likely to attach a greater degree of importance to success in external competition than the head of a boys' or mixed department. Considering the competitiveness of male sport, this was a surprising result. Standards of excellence by school teams and individuals in representative sport is to be welcomed and physical education should cater as far as possible for the physically gifted child. Occasionally the success of the first team has served as a barometer of success for the total work of the department. This should not be so, as teachers have a duty to all the children they teach regardless of their level of ability. The establishment and maintenance of school traditions was also linked to this factor entitled 'standards'.

4 The working climate engendered by the physical education department was an important evaluative factor. Enjoyment was often mentioned as an important ingredient by the teachers. The same could also be said for the two major items comprising this factor, namely the working atmosphere and the development of good attitudes. The three items were rated as important by over 95 per cent of the sample and were ranked highest in the list of methods for judging the success of courses. Affective outcomes in physical education are not usually in the forefront of most teachers' thinking, but they figured prominently in this analysis.

5 The acquisition of skill is an intended outcome of any programme. The linking of skill and fitness levels gave rise to the factor named motor development. A prime aim of physical education is to develop the level of skill of all pupils in a range of activities. Closely allied to this is the improvement of fitness levels in terms of endurance, mobility and strength. These two aspects of motor development, skill and fitness, are ranked highly within the aims of the subject. The evaluation of fitness is comparatively simple and easy to administer and it is possible to make comparisons with norm tables compiled in this country and abroad. Development of skill in many activities can also be objectively measured with good use being made of the standards and award schemes of the national bodies of sport.

6 Some Conclusions About Planning and Implementation of the Physical Education Curriculum

The main purpose of this research study was to examine ways in which teachers plan and implement the physical education curriculum in secondary schools. Rather than adopt a single research strategy, an eclectic approach was used and this enabled information to be collected from a variety of sources using different methods. After reviewing what appeared to be the relevant literature and identifying appropriate research areas, the study began in the schools with tape recorded interviews with heads of physical education departments. In the next stage of the research, seventy-one physical education syllabuses were collected and analyzed by the author and three independent judges. From these approaches, a number of important factors and issues emerged. In order to try to ascertain their importance on a wider scale, a questionnaire was constructed, this was then subjected to a pilot study and the revised questionnaire was sent to a representative sample of 793 schools in England and Wales.

The questionnaire was formulated in an attempt to provide some information which might suggest answers to seven major questions which had arisen from the review of literature and the earlier research strategies. Although the results from the questionnaire provide the main findings, the information from the interviews and the examination of syllabuses are also included and interrelated as they make a contribution to a fuller understanding of the issues involved. Tentative answers to these seven questions have emerged and are discussed under each question in turn.

Some tentative answers

Which staff are involved in planning?

As expected, most heads of department played a major part in the planning of physical education courses and 90 per cent of the teachers in the questionnaire sample considered that they fulfilled this role. However, the remaining 10 per cent considered that they played a moderate or minor part in planning. In respect of the involvement of full-time physical education colleagues, departmental heads encouraged their involvement in planning and a full range of consultation was considered to be essential. The importance of a democratic atmosphere was confirmed in the factor analysis of 'Influencing Factors' and proved to be a recurring theme. A lesser degree of consultation took place with the academic staff who taught a few periods of physical education each week. Almost half were rarely or never involved. In instances where colleagues had suggested changes to the programme, heads of department had generally welcomed this kind of initiative. Most changes, however, were usually achieved through consultations in department meetings or informal discussion, or a combination of both methods. In contrast, about one in twelve departmental heads appeared to make changes without any form of consultation.

Apart from the staff who are involved in the teaching of physical education, the Headteacher and senior staff of the school played an important role in deciding the place of the subject in the school curriculum. This group will probably determine staffing ratios, provision of facilities and equipment, and time-table allocation. All these factors have a profound influence on the physical education curriculum and it would seem important that the head of department represents the subject when this group meets.

A pattern emerges of a wide range of consultation between the head of department and the full-time members of the physical education department, but with less consultation with the academic staff teaching some physical education. It is recommended that every head of department consults with all his colleagues, adopts a professional approach to planning and ensures the plans are executed with high standards. This is one of the best ways of influencing the decisions of the Headteacher and senior staff and ensuring that physical education takes its rightful place in the curriculum.

When is the planning done?

No completely consistent pattern emerged about the timing of planning the physical education curriculum. In the written syllabuses, departmental meetings were hardly mentioned and it was not possible to determine any trends, other than that this item was invariably omitted. During the interviews, it was apparent that departments resorted to a variety of methods for holding and conducting staff discussions. These ranged from regular structured occasions with an agenda, to irregular informal meetings with unstructured discussion. This spectrum was confirmed by the questionnaire data which indicated that approximately half the schools met regularly (either weekly, monthly, termly or annually), while the other half met 'as required'. The most common format for these meetings was either to have a few guidelines or to allow informal discussion. This contrasted with approximately a quarter of the schools who did adopt a formal agenda. The meetings were invariably held outside normal timetabled hours, except in some schools where the organization allocated timetabled periods for this purpose.

In an attempt to interpret these results concerning the regularity of meetings for curriculum planning in physcial education they may possibly be considered at three levels. Firstly, there is the consideration of the total physical education syllabus for the school. This could be reviewed by the full department at least once a year. The syllabus provides a central focus for the work and a sense of direction for the staff. An annual meeting to ensure the full commitment of the department to the implementation of the syllabus would seem to be advisable. The second level is related to the schemes of work in the different activities. These usually last for several weeks and it would seem reasonable to discuss courses of this nature before and after completion. This would necessitate meetings being held termly or half-termly. Thirdly, there are the day-to-day problems encountered in all schools which may require more frequent meetings (perhaps every two to three weeks) to ensure the smooth running of the department. These levels of structuring would determine the nature of the items to be included on the agenda and, to some extent, the type of discussion. For example, items concerned with changes in the syllabus could be formally minuted and executed, whereas items related to more minor problems could be dealt with informally. The conduct of meetings will depend, to some extent, on the personalities involved. What is essential is that the physical education staff do meet collectively on a regular basis to discuss the curriculum.

Which factors influence planning?

The interviews had suggested a number of factors which were important in planning. These included the availability of adequate facilities and the allocation of timetabled periods, and both were considered to be critical by nearly all the sixteen teachers. Confirmation of their importance was established from the questionnaire when these two items were ranked first and second from a list of twenty-three influencing factors. Factor analysis of the twenty-three items produced seven factors. The first was named 'school climate'. Items which made a major contribution related to the traditions of the school and the attitudes of staff to physical education. In particular, this included the support and help offered by male colleagues from other departments. The second factor was related to progression and assessment procedures and was named 'subject procedures'. Factors three and four emphasized the use of 'community' and 'school resources' and these included physical as well as material resources. The fifth factor was named 'societal values' and this introduced a much wider influencing factor. Factor six, 'democratic atmosphere', highlighted the need for democratic discussion within the department, and the final factor emphasized the importance of 'children's abilities and interests'.

General trends, such as staffing levels and financial allocation, can be identified and these will be important to the planning in all schools. At the same time, there will be some factors, for example, community resources, which will have more or less importance according to the particular school. It would, therefore, be unwise to be prescriptive in this area. It is only possible to suggest factors which may influence planning and then allow the teachers to make their own interpretations based on their knowledge of the school.

There was an equal division of opinion about the co-operative planning of the boys' and girls' programmes in mixed schools. The interviews indicated that all eight male heads of department regarded the curriculum as a whole and not as two separate parts, while all eight women teachers reported a completely separate planning procedure. The same trend was confirmed from the questionnaire where the data reached the 1 per cent level of statistical significance. From the mixed schools in this sample, about half planned with all their colleagues, whilst the rest planned independently. The syllabuses that were analyzed made few references to integrated programmes and some schools provided a separate syllabus for the boys' and girls' departments.

Irrespective of the type of department, there was almost total agreement about a compulsory common core of work during the first three years. In the following year, a marked change occurred when almost half the curriculum time was devoted to some choice within the programme. This progressively increased the longer the pupils remained in school, and in the sixth form the optional activities totally dominated the curriculum.

In summary, a number of specific factors have tentatively been identified which may influence planning, but the importance placed on each one will vary according to the needs and resources of the individual school and this can only be decided by the teachers in the specific situation. In mixed schools, it appears that many of the boys' and girls' departments are planning their programmes separately. Whether the staff have made a conscious decision to plan in this way, or whether it has been the accepted pattern in the school which has become a tradition, is not clear. Inevitably, some degree of co-operation is necessary from the purely logistical organization of facilities. However, consideration should also be given to activities where boys and girls can work together and this may be particularly appropriate to the optional activities programme in the senior school.

What methods are used in planning?

The three separate aspects of the study all investigated the methods adopted by teachers in the planning of their syllabuses. A comparison of results from these strategies revealed a number of discrepancies. In the discussions, all the teachers considered that some guidelines to planning would be helpful as few had seen any other physical education syllabuses or received constructive advice and feedback about their own syllabuses. This contrasted markedly with the questionnaire data which suggested a wide range of consultation.

However, the analysis of the syllabuses in this study did not reflect this width of consultation and there was much left to be desired in relation to content and presentation. The reasons for these differences are not immediately apparent and warrant further investigation. For example, a series of selected interviews from the questionnaire sample which allowed in-depth discussion might throw some light on the nature and extent of the consultations.

It did not prove possible to obtain a national sample of syllabuses. This suggested that either the schools were reluctant to make them available or that they did not exist. In contrast, all teachers who were interviewed stated there was a written syllabus available in the school. Similarly, 91 per cent of the questionnaire returns replied positively when asked if an offical written syllabus was in existence. It is possible that there may have been some misinterpretations about what actually comprised a syllabus. Certainly, some teachers considered schemes of work relating to the subject content to represent the syllabus, whereas others presented their syllabus in a much wider educational context and confined statements about the content of practical areas to an appendix.

The discussions with teachers revealed some uncertainty about the main areas to be included in the presentation and planning of a syllabus. The same trend was also apparent in the examination of syllabuses. For example, aspects such as aims of the subject, staffing responsibilities, extra-curricular activities and evaluation procedures were usually omitted. Because of these omissions, a false impression of the work and planning in the department was presented. No systematic approach to planning was apparent and this supported the similar trend reported by Taylor (1970).

Once a syllabus has been written, it should be constantly under review. It transpired that nearly all the teachers had carried out some revision during the past two or three years. In particular, heads of department welcomed constructive suggestions from their colleagues as they considered it gave the staff a more personal and responsible role in planning. Indeed some staff were given responsibility for writing sections of the syllabus relating to activities in which they had a specialist interest.

It appeared that many teachers adopted an analytic approach to the time allocated to physical education as almost two-thirds of the sample from the questionnaire had conducted an analysis of the time allocated to each aspect of the subject termly, annually and over the whole curriculum. This contrasted with an earlier finding when, during the interviews, only one teacher stated that he had conducted such an analysis. Criticism is often levelled at the proliferation of activities and lack of study in depth in physical education. An analysis of the time allocation may be worthwhile as it can reveal the apportionment to each activity and give some indication whether any depth of understanding and development of skill is possible.

Contrary to Kane's (1974) findings which reported almost two-thirds of the physical education departments in his sample being involved in interdisciplinary study to some extent, the present study revealed that little integrated work was undertaken with other departments in the schools, although there were occasional references made to collaborative work with science and drama. There was, however, a greater likelihood that staff would make an attempt to integrate within the subject by planning for links between the different activities in physical education and most teachers stated that they were making some attempt to do this. However, there were no references to these links in the written syllabuses and the exact nature of the integration was not apparent.

The importance of planned and logical progression within the syllabus was discussed and most teachers attempted to achieve progression during the first three years of the programme. Nevertheless, there were exceptions where the planning was less specific. For example, there was less coherence and structure about the fifth and sixth form programmes. Many of the progressions were linked to the more objective aspects of the subject such as athletics, games and swimming, where it was easier to monitor the stages of skilled development. This contrasted with such expressive areas as gymnastics and dance, where the analysis of the syllabuses and the discussions with teachers indicated less specific planning. It was also apparent that over three-quarters of the sample from the questionnaire gave more thought to planning progression in the common core of work than in the optional activities programme. This should not be the case as all aspects of the work are equally important. Thus, a pattern seemed to emerge which indicated a greater commitment to planning and progression in the earlier stages of the secondary school physical education curriculum and this may have been at the expense of the optional activities programme in the senior school.

The above results indicate that a wide variety of methods are used when the physical education syllabus is planned. Some of the syllabuses appear to be effective whereas others leave a great deal to be desired. A complete spectrum of documentation was revealed from those with a detailed and clear exposition of the work in a department to others which adopted a brief and cursory approach. There appeared to be some confusion over what should actually be included in a syllabus and there is an obvious need to bring some kind of order and systematization to this totally diverse approach. In particular, clarification is required about the place of 'syllabuses' for the different activities in physical education. Whilst a brief indication about subject content in an area may be appropriately placed in the main text of a syllabus, details of the specific content of a practical area may best be documented in an appendix.

An annual review of the syllabus by the department should ensure that the curriculum is kept up-to-date. This kind of decision-making would go some way to foster a collective responsibility towards its effective implementation. Indeed the practice of delegating areas of the syllabus to staff with a particular expertise would be one to be recommended. This type of review should include an overview of the total programme. This could then incorporate an analysis of the time devoted to each practical area and its placing throughout the physical education curriculum, as well as an examination of possible links between the various activities. In particular, the coherence between the common core and optional activities programme needs to be clear and a logical progression should be evident throughout.

What is the purpose of planning?

Many curriculum theorists would agree that aims and objectives, content, teaching method and evaluation, are important factors in curriculum planning and they should be reflected in all planning procedures. The extent to which physical education teachers considered these factors to be important was probed in two ways. Firstly, three independent judges conducted an analysis of seventy-one syllabuses, and secondly, approximately six hundred heads of department, in the questionnaire, were asked to make a self-rating of their own syllabus. Although the two groups were analyzing different syllabuses, a clear pattern appeared to emerge. This showed that the largest proportion of the syllabus was allocated to the content and subject matter to be taught in physical education, less emphasis being placed on aims and objectives and teaching method, with evaluation being rarely mentioned. Although the trend was reasonably consistent between the two analyses, the results of the self-rating by the teachers produced a more even distribution between the four factors. A tentative interpretation may indicate that the emphasis teachers place on the different aspects of their syllabus might be interpreted differently by outside observers. However, this needs further investigation and analysis, and discussions with teachers about their own syllabuses would be preferable.

Although general trends were apparent, the range of scores revealed a wide spectrum of opinion. For example, some considered that the statement of aims and objectives to be of no importance at all, whereas others considered such a statement to represent the total syllabus. This division of opinion is surprising when over 95 per cent of these teachers rated the aims of physical education as 'very important' or 'important' as an influencing factor.

Most teachers plan, to a greater or lesser extent, a syllabus of work for physical education in their schools. However, an examination of the syllabuses confirmed the suggestion that the presentation is unique to every school. No two syllabuses were presented in the same format. Apart from this diversity of presentation, many syllabuses excluded vital aspects of their programme. Consequently, this gave a false impression of the work that was taking place in the school.

The teachers were asked to rate the importance of fourteen purposes in the planning of the curriculum. Almost all the responses considered the most important items to be related to guiding the physical education staff, providing continuity in learning and teaching, and ensuring that available resources were used efficiently. In addition, the needs of the children, both during and after their school career, figured prominently. A factor analysis of the fourteen items resulted in the production of four factors. The first and largest factor was named 'co-ordination and continuity' and related to the efficiency within the department and subject organization. Factor two was related to 'guidance for children' and factor three was concerned with 'children's needs'. Factor four was named 'subject guide for staff' and linked items which described guidance for the subject as well as for the staff.

The results in this section pinpoint the prominence of subject content and the relatively insignificant part played by evaluation procedures in planning physical education programmes. In spite of these trends, there were a large number of variations in the presentation of syllabuses. It would not be recommended that all syllabuses should be identical. This would be both unrealistic and inappropriate. In general terms, the purpose of any plan should, where appropriate, include statements about the aims and objectives the subject hopes to achieve, the content to be included, the methods to be used and, finally, an evaluation to determine the extent to which the plan has been successful. The fact that these major areas are not reflected in some planning procedures warrants further investigation. Any plan should ensure that there is co-ordination and continuity both for the subject and for the staff, and this was revealed as a major factor in the analysis. This attempt to achieve coherence would then assist teachers to plan effectively.

How is the planning communicated?

Any plan has to be communicated to those members of staff who are involved in teaching the subject. The interviews suggested that heads of department mainly communicated with their staff in two ways, namely, through the written syllabus and departmental meetings. This trend was supported by the results from the questionnaire. However, it is important to note that one-third of the sample did not distribute a copy of the complete syllabus and that many teachers (almost one-fifth) did not receive a copy of those aspects of the syllabus which they taught. As nearly all schools stated there was a written syllabus available, this suggests that there was only a single copy in some departments. A different pattern was evident for the academic staff who taught some physical education. Almost half received a copy of the entire written syllabus or the relevant parts of it, but a more common form of communication was through verbal guidelines.

The totality and coherence of planning is the responsibility of the head of department. It transpired that this responsibility was taken seriously as nearly all the teachers replied that they carried out checks, either frequently or infrequently, to ensure that courses taught by colleagues had been carried out in accordance with the overall plan.

The production of any syllabus indicates that decisions have been made by someone about what is to be taught and when it is to be included in the programme. Within this framework, teachers appeared to have a great deal of autonomy about their teaching style. The extent to which a particular teaching style was imposed for the different activities showed that over three-quarters of the heads of department in the questionnaire sample tended not to specify the style to be adopted by colleagues. In addition, age and sex differences were not found to be statistically significant. These findings indicate that the strategies teachers adopt in their teaching is mainly left to their professional judgement and not imposed by the head of department.

As well as communicating with the staff in the department, some communication must also take place with the pupils, and the extent to which teachers communicated to children the long-term aims of physical education and the short-term objectives of a course was probed. In the interviews, most teachers stated that they did not deliberately communicate the aims of the subject to the children and gave the impression that when they did communicate them, it was done incidentally and infrequently. A slightly different picture emerged for the shorter-term objectives which revealed a greater likelihood of the children being told the objectives before starting a block of work. This trend was confirmed by the questionnaire results for all teachers in the different types of school in England and Wales, and may partly be explained by the fact that objectives are more tangible than aims and can be realized more readily. Consequently, they would have more immediate meaning for pupils.

The data from the questions in this section has indicated the importance of the syllabus for the purpose of communication. If a written syllabus is available, it would seem advisable that a copy of the document, or the relevant sections, is given to the staff who are responsible for the teaching. Not only is the written word less likely to be misinterpreted, but if safety is involved, for example in swimming or outdoor activities, it is essential the safety requirements are set out in the clearest possible way. Additionally, all curriculum plans should have coherence and the contribution each part makes to the total picture should be clear. This will go some way to ensure that staff do not teach in isolated pockets and the curriculum is planned as a whole unit.

There appears to be some lack of communication with the pupils concerning the purposes of the subject as well as the objectives of particular courses. In terms of effective communication this is to be regretted. Whilst it may not always be possible, or indeed advisable, to specify aims and objectives, a clear statement at the outset about the intended learning outcomes would generally be considered helpful and give a sense of direction to the pupils' efforts. This is a neglected aspect of communication and could well benefit from further investigation.

How is the success of the planning judged?

One of the ways in which teachers judged the success of their planning was reflected in the progress made by pupils. In relation to the individual, almost every teacher took into account the efforts pupils put into their work and the development of skill and ability levels when they assessed progress. In the recording of development in these areas, evaluation procedures appeared to adopt both a norm and a criterion based approach. Norms of skill level in many activities could be measured against objective criteria such as time and distance. This type of measurement was supplemented by teachers' subjective opinions and the fact that almost every questionnaire response referred to the value teachers placed on individual effort supported the notion of criterion referenced evaluation. In addition, the importance teachers attached to the physical development of pupils was examined. The questionnaire results showed that less than half the heads of department incorporated standards of physical fitness as part of their evaluation and this aspect was not accorded the same prominence as ability and effort. These findings are consistent with the results of Carroll's (1976) study.

The methods used to record individual progress of pupils varied enormously. In the interviews, teachers referred to the use of card-index filing systems and departmental books for recording purposes, but the majority relied upon the school report. The same trend was also apparent from the questionnaire data and it transpired that more than half the departmental heads did not keep a systematic record in the department. For these teachers, the termly or annual school report was considered to be a sufficient record. Although the school report was the most common method of recording, one-fifth of the questionnaire sample expressed reservations about its format and regarded it as restricted and inadequate.

Of the four main components of curriculum planning, namely, aims and objectives, content, teaching method and evaluation, the evaluation component received the least emphasis. The overall impression from the interviews was that the teachers were vague about their evaluation procedures. This was partly confirmed from the results of the questionnaire, which indicated that more than half the teachers were not regularly and systematically evaluating their original aims. There was, however, a greater likelihood of evaluation being used to influence the planning of future courses, and two-thirds indicated that they used evaluation for this purpose. While this is to be commended, it still left a high proportion using evaluation procedures infrequently. The evidence tends to suggest that the central role played by evaluation in the 'rational curriculum planning' process is not supported by the majority of teachers in the present investigation.

The teachers were asked to indicate the degree of importance they attached to fifteen methods of evaluation for judging the success of their curriculum. Almost without exception, the greatest importance was attached to the affective areas concerned with the development of good attitudes and enjoyment. The improvement of skill levels in a good working atmosphere, and participation in extra-curricular activities and post school recreation were also rated highly. Two other high scoring variables referred to social competence and the attainment of standards of physical fitness. A factor analysis of the fifteen items produced five factors. The first factor was named 'aesthetic and social appreciation' and derived its name from the loadings on two items with these titles. Factor two, 'leisure participation', showed an emphasis on post school and extra-curricular activity. The third factor, 'standards', was concerned with the standards within the physical education department and factor four, 'climate', related to the working atmosphere and development of good attitudes. The last factor emphasized skill and fitness levels and was named 'motor development'.

The importance of school-based evaluation with the 'Teacher as Researcher' has been stressed. Pring (1978) suggested six procedures which might be used for this purpose. These were the use of interaction analysis, participant observation, audio-visual aids, first hand reports, pupils' opinions and triangulation techniques. No evidence was revealed from the interviews with teachers or the analysis of syllabuses which indicated that any of these procedures are being currently used in schools. Thus, it appears that these particular methods of evaluation are being ignored by most physical education teachers in secondary schools.

The results in this section tend to suggest that teachers consider the affective areas to be slightly more important than the development of skill and physical fitness levels. In addition, teachers appear to place more emphasis on ability and effort than on physical development when recording individual progress. With the advent of national fitness norms in this country, and the recent emphasis towards health and fitness, perhaps future evaluation will pay more attention to these areas.

Teachers do have a responsibility for monitoring individual progress and this should be done as efficiently as possible. A simple card-index system which allowed ease of recording should be comparatively easy to plan and would provide a central point to record individual development. Looking to the future, with the development of modern technology, it may be possible to use computer facilities to store and record details of pupils' progress throughout the school in all subjects on the curriculum.

If evaluation is to be useful in planning, then it should give an indication of the measure of success in achieving the stated aims of the subject and the objectives of a course, as well as providing feedback relevant to future planning. At present, there is little evidence to suggest that there is much school-based evaluation in operation. Evaluation appears to be a relatively neglected area in physical education and there is a need for future development in this aspect of planning.

Curriculum Planning

The question arises, therefore, how the evidence produced in this study relates to the totality of curriculum planning in physical education in secondary schools. There was no evidence to suggest that teachers plan their curriculum in accordance with the linear or cyclical models as suggested, for example, by

Tyler (1949) and Wheeler (1967). Indeed, many of the syllabuses made no reference at all to aims and objectives or to evaluation procedures. The dominance of the content of the subject suggests that this may well be the starting point for many teachers when they plan the curriculum and supports the similar trends identified by Taylor (1970) and Zahorik (1975).

Any suggestion that physical education planning is becoming objective and narrow in its approach is not apparent from the results of this study. Clegg's (1975) warning that accountability might demand such an approach in this country is not supported. There is no evidence to suggest that objectives were being specified in such detail that knowledge and skills were becoming 'trivialized' and isolated. In addition, the lack of emphasis on evaluation procedures dispelled the notion that teachers were overemphasizing an objectives approach in the pursuit of accountability.

The Schools Council Enquiry entitled *Physical Education in the Secondary School* suggested that there were nine main aims or long-term objectives in physical education. In talking to teachers about their own aims, the four areas mentioned most frequently, and which overlapped with the aims of the Schools Council Enquiry, were the development of motor skills, recreation for leisure, health and fitness and socialization. There were, however, five aims which were only occasionally mentioned by a few teachers and these related to self-realization, emotional, moral, cognitive and aesthetic development. A tentative interpretation would suggest that not all the main aims of the subject considered to be important by the theorists are also deemed to be important by practising teachers. In addition, it is noticeable that the teachers emphasized the more overt aims to the exclusion of the more covert areas.

In general, there appears to be a considerable gap between the manner in which some curriculum theorists suggest planning should be carried out and the way in which practising teachers actually plan physical education programmes. Further studies are indicated which would go some way towards closing this gap.

Summary of the Main Findings

On the basis of the evidence from this study, the following statements can tentatively be made about the planning and implementation of the physical education curriculum.

1 Heads of department play a major role in planning and consult widely with their physical education colleagues. A lesser degree of consultation takes place with staff in other departments who teach some physical education each week.

2 Different types of departmental meetings are held which range from regular structured meetings with an agenda to irregular informal meetings with unstructured discussion.

3 Seven factors were identified which influenced the planning of the physical education curriculum and are listed in relative order of importance and size. These were named:

a) School climate,
b) Subject procedures,
c) Community resources,
d) School resources,
e) Societal values,
f) Democratic atmosphere,
g) Children's abilities and interests.

4 In mixed schools, almost half the departments plan the boys' and the girls' physical education programmes together, and the remainder plan separately.

5 Almost all schools plan a compulsory common core of work during the first three years, and this is followed by progressively increased choice in a range of activities the longer the pupils remain in school.

6 The analysis of seventy-one syllabuses revealed:

a) great diversity in the presentation and content,
b) that many areas of work are frequently omitted and the syllabus is not a true reflection of the work of the department.

7 Nearly all teachers regularly reviewed the syllabus.

8 Most teachers analyze the time allocation to each aspect of the curriculum in order to examine the balance of the programme.

9 Approximately nine out of ten teachers are attempting to integrate within the subject by planning for links between the different activities that comprise physical education.

10 Three-quarters of the teachers spend more time planning the common core of work than the optional activities programme.

11 Four factors were identified for the purpose of planning the physical education curriculum and are listed in relative order of importance and size. These were named:

a) Co-ordination and continuity.
b) Guidance for children,
c) Children's needs,
d) Subject guide for staff.

12 The most common methods used by most heads of department to communicate their plan was through the entire written syllabus and regular verbal guidelines.

13 Nearly all heads of department checked that the physical education syllabus was being implemented according to the plan. Almost half checked frequently and the remainder infrequently.

14 Most teachers have a great deal of autonomy in planning their own teaching strategies and particular teaching styles are rarely imposed by heads of department.

15 Most teachers communicate to children the short-term objectives of a course more frequently than the long-term aims of the subject.

16 Most teachers, when recording pupils' progress, accorded greater importance to ability and effort than to physical fitness.

17 Most heads of department do not keep records of pupils' progress in the department, but rely upon the school report for this purpose.

18 Most heads of department do not regularly and systematically evaluate their original aims.

19 Most heads of department regularly use the results of their evaluation to influence the planning of future courses.

20 Five factors were identified for judging the success of a course and are listed in relative order of importance and size. These were named:

a) Aesthetic and social appreciation,
b) Leisure participation,
c) Standards,
d) Climate,
e) Motor development.

21 No evidence was revealed which suggested that teachers are 'acting as researchers' in school-based evaluation.

22 General trends show that teachers place most emphasis on the content of programmes; less emphasis is placed on aims and objectives and teaching method; and any form of evaluation is regarded as least important.

23 Teachers do not plan in accordance with linear or cyclical models proposed by some curriculum theorists.

24 Teachers are not adopting narrow and objective approaches to planning in the pursuit of accountability.

25 Not all the aims of physical education as proposed by curriculum theorists are considered to be important by practising teachers.

Future Research

The study has raised a number of issues worthy of further research. Rather than consider each issue individually, a number of main areas have been identified. It is ten years since the Schools Council (1970–71) carried out a Physical Education Enquiry which 'was intended to provide the basis for a curriculum development project'. This has not been followed by a major curriculum study in spite of the submission of concrete proposals. The information from this Schools Council study and the present investigation would provide a sound basis from which to embark on other projects.

Regardless of whether a project is nationally or locally based, it must have as one of its main aims the intention of providing physical education teachers with constructive suggestions and help in the overall planning and implementation of the curriculum. The relationship between curriculum theory and practice does not appear to be particularly strong and there should be a deliberate attempt to establish closer links. To be effective, a considerable number of teachers, lecturers and advisers need to be involved at all stages. At the present time there are a number of isolated groups working under different auspices who are doing excellent work examining various aspects of curriculum planning. The sharing of the information, knowledge and ideas gained in these working groups could provide a valuable source of background material which could give a direct input into schools and initial and in-serivce training structures.

Comparatively little research has been based in schools and there is a need to discuss with individual staff in their schools and engage groups of teachers in open discussion. The free exchange of ideas, syllabuses and even staffing within educational authorities would be necessary to generate interest and innovation. A number of documented case studies which identify 'good practice' in schools would help to isolate those variables which are important to efficient and efffective teaching. It would also give insight into the organization and working of well run departments. This kind of documentation is not currently available in physical education.

Another major task would be to devize experimental units of work and it is suggested that these could take two forms. The first would involve the preparation of appropriate learning experiences and a framework for evaluation in a variety of activities in, for example, athletics, dance, games, gymnastics and swimming. Additionally, human movement, as a field of study, lends itself naturally to an inter-disciplinary approach, and a second investigation could examine such topics as, 'Biomechanics in Sport', 'Fitness and Health', 'Women and Sport' and 'Aesthetics and Sport'. The experimental work would have to be tested in schools and discussed and modified where necessary. It may also be advisable to have supplementary visual material in the form of videotapes supported by audiotapes and explanatory booklets.

In this study, factor analysis techniques were used on three occasions in an attempt to identify the influencing factors, the purposes of planning and the ways in which teachers judge the success of their courses. In all three instances, the resulting factors can only be considered to be tentative. There is now a need to compile a substantial number of items under each factor and submit these to the physical education profession to establish their relative importance.

The evaluation component in physical education appears to be the least developed aspect of planning and warrants special attention if school-based evaluation is to become a realistic possibility in the future. Techniques and ideas need to be developed which, with documented examples, would provide teachers with some potential guidelines.

Some developments about the analysis of the teaching situation are also necessary. These developments could incorporate the use of the video tape recorder and even more sophisticated technology such as wide-angled lenses which record the movements of all the class, and zoom lenses which can focus on 'critical incidents' or individual children. These refinements would give additional dimensions to the total analysis. However, they must not become too technical otherwise they would defeat the purpose of the exercise which is to provide a method of analysis for teachers in schools. Recently, Anderson (1980) has made some positive suggestions for teachers of physical education which could assist them in analyzing aspects of teaching such as, student and teacher behaviour, teacher-student interaction, and evaluating the relationship between the plans and eventual outcomes. Although based on data from the USA, Anderson's suggestions are worthy of detailed study and application in this country.

The abilities, attitudes and interests of pupils need to be taken into consideration in the construction of a syllabus to ensure that it is relevant to them. In a secondary education that may span seven years, the needs and feelings of pupils will inevitably change and the physical education curriculum planners must be aware of the nature of these changes and take suitable steps to cater for them. Very little evidence has been obtained about the pupils' feelings towards physical education and it would seem important that their views are considered with regard to curriculum content, especially in the later years at school. As well as this, it would be revealing to discover their views on the perceived outcomes they consider the physical education programme has achieved. Any discrepancies existing between the theorists, the teachers and the pupils about the intended outcomes of the subject would suggest a lack of clarity in communication and the need for more precise planning.

The dissemination of the results of these studies must be deliberately planned if they are to have any impact on the teaching profession. This could give rise to a number of discussion documents and audio-visual material on curriculum planning and development which could serve as guidelines for seminar material at initial and in-service courses. This is a time of enormous change and innovation in education and teachers need to be aware of developments that are taking place. It is incumbent on every physical education teacher to plan an effective programme of work and a knowledge of other studies should help him to make informed and educated decisions. Ultimately, it is the children who are taught who will receive the benefit.

Appendices

Appendix A:
Interviews with Teachers: Discussion Questions

1. Planning of courses

How do you plan your courses?
What factors do you take into account?
Are there any basic principles or criteria to be followed?
Does the department have clear guidelines for planning?
Are boys' and girls' programmes planned separately or integrated?
Would you appreciate any guidelines for planning?

Supplementary questions

When was the syllabus formulated/written?
Is the syllabus reviewed regularly?
Is the syllabus discussed by the department?
Do you have regular department meetings?
Are non-PE staff who assist, informed or consulted about the syllabus?

2. Aims and objectives

What are the main aims you hope physical education achieves in your school?
Do you state what you hope to achieve?
Are some aims more important than others?
Do you communicate the aims and objectives of physical education to the children?
How do you cater for individual differences?

Supplementary questions

Are the aims just related to motor skills?
Do you cater specifically for health and fitness?

3. Content

What principles or guidelines do you use when selecting content?
Do you have a compulsory 'common core'?
Do you have a system of optional activities?
Is there a balance between activities?
Has a 'time analysis' been made for each activity?
Are any Award schemes used?

Supplementary questions

Which activities have the greatest/least time allocation?
Which outside authorities influence your choice of content?
Are optional activities compulsory?

4. Learning experiences and teaching method

Do you try to ensure a range of experiences e.g. individual, team, mixed, expressive?
How important is extra-curricular activity?
Is there horizontal planning throughout the year?
Is there vertical planning and progression between years?
Is the department involved in any inter-disciplinary studies?
Do you use different teaching styles, e.g. Direct, Guided Discovery, Problem-Solving, or do you generally adopt the same style?

Supplementary questions

How do you cater for mixed abilities?
Do boys and girls work together at any time?
Have you 'blocked' any of your teaching time?
Are all extra-curricular activities open to all children?

5. Evaluation

How do you judge the success of a course?
Do you try to evaluate your original aims?
Do you record a child's progress? (What, how often and for whom?)

Supplementary questions

Do you discuss standards in the department?

Is staff feedback formal or informal?
Do you judge progress with reference to the individual or group norms?

6. Reactions of teachers

Are there any aspects of planning that you consider to be important which have not been included?
Please give me your frank and honest opinion on my approach to, and conduct of, the discussion.

Appendix B: *Analysis of Physical Education Syllabuses: Analysis 2 Check List*

BOYS ☐ GIRLS ☐ BOYS & GIRLS ☐

Format: Typewritten ☐ Written ☐ Number of pages ☐ SYLLABUS ☐

1.	Introductory statement	1	☐
2.	Staff list and qualifications	2	☐
3.	Job specification	3	☐
4.	Visiting coaches	4	☐
5.	Probationary teacher guidance	5	☐
6.	Student teacher guidance	6	☐
7.	Department meetings	7	☐
8.	Finance	8	☐
9.	Facilities	9	☐
10.	Lists of equipment	10	☐
11.	Clothing	11	☐
12.	Showering	12	☐
13.	Time allocation	13	☐
14.	Diagrammatic presentation of syllabus	14	☐
15.	Common core	15	☐
16.	Optional activities	16	☐
17.	Award schemes	17	☐
18.	Extra-curricular activities	18	☐
19.	Competition – internal	19	☐

20. Competition – external .... 20 ☐
21. Medical service/remedials .... 21 ☐
22. Health education .... 22 ☐
23. Safety .... 23 ☐
24. Audio-visual aids .... 24 ☐
25. Bibliography .... 25 ☐

Comments ....
....
....

Appendix C:
The Planning and Implementation of The Physical Education Curriculum: Teacher Questionnaire

This questionnaire has been constructed in order to gather information about the ways in which secondary school teachers plan and implement the physical education curriculum. Successful methods for doing this vary and there are no right or wrong ways.

Knowledge of the approach to planning and teaching physical education in your school will form an important part of the information being gathered. The data collected from this survey will provide useful guidelines to teachers of physical education.

Your answers will be treated confidentially. Neither the name of the school nor the identity of the respondents will be revealed to anyone in any way.

THE PLANNING AND IMPLEMENTATION OF
THE PHYSICAL EDUCATION CURRICULUM

To be completed by the Head of the Physical Education Department

> For most questions, boxes are provided for answers. Please give the necessary information by placing a tick (√) in the appropriate box or boxes. For the remaining questions, separate instructions are given with each question.
>
> N.B. All references to courses and planning throughout this questionnaire relate to physical education.

PLEASE LEAVE THIS MARGIN BLANK

Card No. 1

☐☐☐ 1 2 3

I. Biographical information

1. These answers are being completed by:

   Head of boys' physical education --- ☐ 1

   Head of girls' physical education --- ☐ 2

   Head of boys' and girls' physical education --- ☐ 3

   ☐ 4

2. Sex of respondent:

   Male --- ☐ 1

   Female --- ☐ 2

   ☐ 5

3. To which age range do you belong?

   21–30 years --- ☐ 1

   31–40 years --- ☐ 2

   41–50 years --- ☐ 3

   Over 51 years --- ☐ 4

   ☐ 6

4. How many years have you been teaching as a specialist physical education teacher? (Please state the number) --- ___ years

   ☐☐ 7 8

5. Type of school in which you are now teaching:

   Comprehensive --- ☐ 1

   Grammar --- ☐ 2

   Secondary Modern/High --- ☐ 3

   ☐ 9

PLEASE LEAVE THIS MARGIN BLANK

6. Size of school:
(Please state the number of pupils) --- —— pupils

☐☐☐☐ 10 11 12 13

7. Is your school single sexed or mixed?

Single sex (boys) --- ☐ 1

Single sex (girls) --- ☐ 2

Mixed (boys and girls) --- ☐ 3

☐ 14

II. Staff involvement

8. What part do you play in the planning of courses?

Major part --- ☐ 1

Moderate part --- ☐ 2

Minor part --- ☐ 3

☐ 15

9. How much are full-time staff in the physical education department involved in planning?

A great deal --- ☐ 1

Often --- ☐ 2

Occasionally --- ☐ 3

Rarely --- ☐ 4

Never --- ☐ 5

☐ 16

10. How much are full-time academic staff, who teach some physical education, involved in planning?

A great deal --- ☐ 1

Often --- ☐ 2

Occasionally --- ☐ 3

Rarely --- ☐ 4

Never --- ☐ 5

☐ 17

PLEASE LEAVE THIS MARGIN BLANK

11. How are changes in the curriculum implemented?

		Yes	No	
Imposed by Head of Department	---	☐	☐	☐ 18
Through departmental meetings	---	☐	☐	☐ 19
Through informal discussion	---	☐	☐	☐ 20
Other (please specify)	---	☐	☐	☐ 21

---

12. Who decides the place of physical education in the school curriculum?

Headteacher --- ☐ 1

Headteacher & Deputy Head --- ☐ 2

Headteacher and Heads of Department --- ☐ 3

Headteacher and staff --- ☐ 4

Other (please specify) --- ☐ 5 ☐ 22

III. Timing of planning

13. Are Departmental meetings held:

Weekly --- ☐ 1

Monthly --- ☐ 2

Termly --- ☐ 3

Annually --- ☐ 4

Seldom --- ☐ 5

Never --- ☐ 6

As required --- ☐ 7

Other (please specify) --- ☐ 8

☐ 23

PLEASE LEAVE THIS MARGIN BLANK

14. Are departmental meetings held in:

		Yes	No	
Time-tabled time	---			☐ 24
Non time-tabled time	---			☐ 25

15. Are most of your departmental meetings carried out:

		Yes	No	
With an agenda	---			☐ 26
With a few guidelines	---			☐ 27
In an informal way	---			☐ 28

IV. Influencing factors

16. Listed below are some factors which may influence your planning of the physical education curriculum. We are interested in the importance that you attach to these factors on a scale that ranges from 'Very Important' to 'Not Important at all'. You are asked to place a tick (√) in the appropriate space, e.g. if you consider 'abilities of children' to be neither important nor unimportant you would record as follows:

Influencing Factor	Very Impor-tant	Import tant	Neither Impor-tant nor Unim-portant	Unim-portant	Not Impor-tant at all
Abilities of children			√		

Please record similarly against the following factors:

	Influencing Factor	Very Impor-tant	Impor-tant	Neither Impor-tant nor Unim-portant	Unim-portant	Not Impor-tant at all	PLEASE LEAVE THIS MARGIN BLANK
1	Interests & abilities of PE staff						29
2	Help offered by non-PE staff						30
3	Use of external qualified coaches						31
4	Adequate facilities						32
5	Adequate financial provision						33
6	Use of local community facilities						34
7	Time-table allocation						35
8	Traditions of school						36
9	Attitude of school staff to PE						37
10	Ability to offer choice at some stage						38
11	Sport in local area						39
12	Democratic discus-sion with PE staff						40
13	Cultural values						41
14	Aims of physical education						42
15	Needs of society						43
16	Suggestions by PE advisers						44
17	Needs of other school subjects						45
18	Personal needs of child						46
19	Range of abilities within classes						47
20	Interests of children						48
21	Age of children						49
22	Assessment procedures						50
23	Logical progression						51

PLEASE LEAVE THIS MARGIN BLANK

17. Do the male and female staff plan the boys' and girls' programmes:

Separately --- ☐ 1
Together --- ☐ 2
Not applicable --- ☐ 3 ☐ 52

18. Do you have a common core of activities which all the children of any one year group must follow?

Yes --- ☐ 1
No --- ☐ 2 ☐ 53

If Yes, does this apply to:	Yes	No	
1st Year (11–12 years) ---			☐ 54
2nd Year (12–13 years) ---			☐ 55
3rd Year (13–14 years) ---			☐ 56
4th Year (14–15 years) ---			☐ 57
5th Year (15–16 years) ---			☐ 58
6th Year (16+ years) ---			☐ 59

19. During optional activities are the children under instruction?

Almost always --- ☐ 1
Usually --- ☐ 2
Occasionally --- ☐ 3
Rarely --- ☐ 4
Never --- ☐ 5 ☐ 60

V. Method of planning

PLEASE LEAVE THIS MARGIN BLANK

20. Is there an official written physical education syllabus in your school?

Yes	--- ☐ 1		
No	--- ☐ 2		☐ 61

21. When you planned your syllabus did you:

		Yes	No	
Refer to books	---			☐ 62
Refer to articles	---			☐ 63
Take external advice	---			☐ 64
Refer to college course	---			☐ 65
Refer to other P.E. syllabuses	---			☐ 66
Obtain ideas from in-service courses	---			☐ 67
Use your own ideas	---			☐ 68
Other (please specify)	---			☐ 69

---

22. Has your physical education syllabus been revised:

During the last academic year	--- ☐ 1	
During the last 2–3 years	--- ☐ 2	
During the last 4–5 years	--- ☐ 3	
More than 5 years ago	--- ☐ 4	
Not revised at all	--- ☐ 5	☐ 70

23. If the syllabus has been revised, which person/s were involved?

		Yes	No	
Head of Department	---			☐ 71
Whole department	---			☐ 72
Section from the department	---			☐ 73
Exteenal advisers	---			☐ 74

PLEASE LEAVE THIS MARGIN BLANK

24. Do you periodically analyze the number of hours devoted to each physical education activity in your syllabus?

Yes --- ☐ 1
No --- ☐ 2

☐ 75

25. Do you plan for links between the different activities in physical education?

A great deal --- ☐ 1
A little --- ☐ 2
Not at all --- ☐ 3

☐ 76

26. Do you give more thought to the planning of progressions for the 'common core' of work than for the optional activities?

Much more --- ☐ 1
Slightly more --- ☐ 2
Same --- ☐ 3
Slightly less --- ☐ 4
Much less --- ☐ 5

☐ 77

PLEASE LEAVE THIS MARGIN BLANK

Card No. 2

VI. Purpose of planning

27. Aims and objectives, content, method and evaluation are generally recognized as the four most important factors in curriculum planning. You are asked to judge the proportion of your syllabus which is associated with these areas by allocating some part of 100% to each (total must equal 100). In order to obtain a qualitative judgement, the proportion that you allocate is to be guided by the emphasis given to the statements rather than the number of words written e.g. if your syllabus was equally related to all four areas you would record 25 against each area.

1 2 3

Aims and objectives --- ☐ 4 5 6

Content --- ☐ 7 8 9

Teaching method --- ☐ 10 11 12

Evaluation --- ☐ 13 14 15

28. Listed below are some of the purposes that the planning of the curriculum may have for you. We are interested in the importance that you attach to these factors on a scale that ranges from 'Very Important' to 'Not Important at all'. You are asked to place a tick (√) in the space that reflects your viewpoint.

	Purpose	Very Impor-tant	Impor-tant	Neither Impor-tant nor Unim-portant	Unim-portant	Not Impor-tant at all	PLEASE LEAVE THIS MARGIN BLANK
1	As a guide to the PE staff						☐ 16
2	As a guide to the subject						☐ 17
3	As a way of suggesting teaching methods						☐ 18
4	As a consideration of children's needs whilst at school						☐ 19
5	As a consideration of children's needs once they have left school						☐ 20
6	To ensure efficient use of resources and facilities						☐ 21
7	To ensure continuity in teaching						☐ 22
8	To state the aims of PE						☐ 23
9	As a guide to the children						☐ 24
10	To utilize staff expertise						☐ 25
11	To be consistent with school philosophy						☐ 26
12	To enable Head of Dept. to co-ordinate work						☐ 27
13	To provide suitable learning experiences						☐ 28
14	To ensure adequate evaluation						☐ 29

PLEASE LEAVE THIS MARGIN BLANK

VII. Communication

29. Do you communicate your curriculum plan to colleagues in the physical education department through:

	Yes	No	
Entire written syllabus ---			☐ 30
Parts of the written syllabus ---			☐ 31
Regular verbal guidelines ---			☐ 32
Verbal guidelines at the start of a term ---			☐ 33

30. Do you communicate your curriculum plan to non-physical education staff through:

	Yes	No	
Entire written syllabus ---			☐ 34
Parts of the written syllabus ---			☐ 35
Regular verbal guidelines ---			☐ 36
Verbal guidelines at the start of a term ---			☐ 37

31. If you are responsible for the planning of a course which will be carried out by someone else, do you:

Check frequently that the plan is being implemented --- ☐ 1

Make infrequent checks --- ☐ 2

Make no checks --- ☐ 3 ☐ 38

32. Do you specify a particular teaching style to the different activities in your planning?

Always --- ☐ 1

Fairly often --- ☐ 2

Sometimes --- ☐ 3

Rarely --- ☐ 4

Never --- ☐ 5 ☐ 39

PLEASE LEAVE THIS MARGIN BLANK

33. Do you communicate the long-term aims of physical education to children?

Almost always	--- ☐	1	
Usually	--- ☐	2	
Occasionally	--- ☐	3	
Rarely	--- ☐	4	
Never	--- ☐	5	☐ 40

34. Do you communicate the short-term objectives of a course to children?

Almost always	--- ☐	1	
Usually	--- ☐	2	
Occasionally	--- ☐	3	
Rarely	--- ☐	4	
Never	--- ☐	5	☐ 41

VIII. Evaluation

35. Which of the following methods do you use to record pupils' progress?

	Yes	No	
Termly report ---			☐ 42
Annual report ---			☐ 43
Department book ---			☐ 44
Numerical grades ---			☐ 45
Literal grades ---			☐ 46
Card index filing system ---			☐ 47
Representative honours ---			☐ 48
Other (please specify) ---			☐ 49

PLEASE LEAVE THIS MARGIN BLANK

36. Which of the following do you consider when recording pupils' progress?

		Yes	No	
Ability	---	☐	☐	☐ 50
Effort	---	☐	☐	☐ 51
Physical fitness	---	☐	☐	☐ 52

37. When writing school reports, is the space provided:

Unlimited --- ☐ 1

Restricted but adequate --- ☐ 2

Restricted and inadequate --- ☐ 3 ☐ 53

38. Do you systematically attempt to evaluate your original aims of physical education?

A great deal --- ☐ 1

Often --- ☐ 2

Occasionally --- ☐ 3

Rarely --- ☐ 4

Never --- ☐ 5 ☐ 54

39. Does your evaluation influence the planning of future courses?

Always --- ☐ 1

Fairly often --- ☐ 2

Sometimes --- ☐ 3

Rarely --- ☐ 4

Never --- ☐ 5 ☐ 55

PLEASE LEAVE THIS MARGIN BLANK

40. Listed below are some of the ways in which teachers judge the success of their curriculum planning. We are interested in the importance that you attach to these factors on a scale that ranges from 'Very Important' to 'Not Important at all'. You are asked to place a tick (√) in the space that reflects your viewpoint.

	Method	Very Important	Important	Neither Important nor Unimportant	Unimportant	Not Important at all	
1	Maintaining school traditions						☐ 56
2	Participation in post school recreation						☐ 57
3	Objective measurement						☐ 58
4	Subjective opinion						☐ 59
5	Enjoyment						☐ 60
6	Development of good attitudes						☐ 61
7	Working atmosphere						☐ 62
8	Skill levels						☐ 63
9	Success in external competition						☐ 64
10	Fitness levels						☐ 65
11	Extra-curricular participation						☐ 66
12	Social competence						☐ 67
13	Aesthetic appreciation						☐ 68
14	Parental interest						☐ 69
15	Other teachers' opinions						☐ 70
16	Other (please specify)						☐ 71

THANK YOU FOR YOUR HELP AND CO-OPERATION

Appendix D
Factor Analysis of Influencing Factors, Purposes of Planning and Methods of Evaluation

In order to determine the number and nature of the underlying variables concerning the influencing factors (23 items), purposes of planning (14 items) and methods of evaluation (15 items), the data was normalized and three component analyses were carried out from the intercorrelations of the teachers' responses. The resulting factors were rotated to an orthogonal solution according to the Varimax criterion.

The following factors were produced for the three areas:

i. *Influencing factors*
Seven rotated factors were produced to explain the underlying variables related to the teachers' rating of the 23 items which appear to influence their planning. These were named and accounted for 56% of the variance.

ii. *Purposes of planning*
Four factors were rotated and named to explain the main elements in the teachers' perception of the fourteen items which underlie the purposes of their planning. These four factors accounted for 51% of the variance.

iii. *Methods of evaluation*
Five factors accounting for 54% of the variance were rotated and named to explain teachers' responses to the fifteen items concerning evaluation of the curriculum.

Influencing factors

Table D.1 lists the 23 items and their rotated loadings on the seven factors. The seven factors were identified and subsequently named from the loadings.

Table D.1. Influencing Factors: Variables & Rotated Component Loadings.

Component loadings*

Item	Variable	1	2	3	4	5	6	7
1	Interests & abilities of PE staff	24	02	34	−01	−20	22	05
2	Help offered by non-PE staff	35	−04	36	03	−05	05	−01
3	Use of external qualified coaches	20	14	54	−01	01	07	02
4	Adequate facilities	02	06	09	62	03	01	−01
5	Adequate financial provision	35	05	16	33	18	−13	08
6	Use of local community facilities	−04	05	59	20	24	02	03
7	Timetable allocation	16	28	02	52	02	09	−01
8	Traditions of school	58	11	08	05	−03	06	07
9	Attitude of school staff to PE	72	12	13	05	19	12	06
10	Ability to offer choice at some stage	07	06	24	−02	16	38	17
11	Sport in local area	17	20	26	−06	31	15	04
12	Democratic discussion with PE staff	11	25	08	12	12	68	−02
13	Cultural values	14	27	14	−04	38	34	−05
14	Aims of physical education	−18	29	−16	21	33	31	05
15	Needs of society	04	09	04	14	60	08	10
16	Suggestions by PE advisers	12	42	16	09	11	05	07
17	Needs of other school subjects	33	43	17	−03	32	10	08
18	Personal needs of child	06	25	−06	10	26	14	22
19	Range of abilities within classes	13	03	05	10	07	01	78
20	Interests of children	34	21	13	−21	06	07	37
21	Age of children	−12	10	−02	33	10	06	25
22	Assessment procedures	10	57	11	09	07	13	02
23	Logical progression	−03	58	−12	30	08	13	07
	Cumulative % variance	19.1	28.5	35.1	41.0	46.4	51.3	55.7

* Decimal point omitted; loadings rounded to two places.

Factor 1

A high loading is recorded against item 9, a moderate loading against item 8 and low loadings against items 2, 5, 17 and 20. These variables are concerned with the attitudes and traditions of the school, the support of the staff and the interests of the children. An overall name to describe this factor is *school climate*.

Factor 2

Items 16, 17, 22 and 23 all have moderate loadings on this factor, but the interpretation is not straightforward. It is related to the progression and assessment procedures of the subject as well as the involvement of the teaching staff and physical education advisers. The factor is tentatively named *subject procedures*.

Factor 3

Moderately high loadings (items 3 and 6) are concerned with the use of external qualified coaches and local community facilities. The help offered by non physical education staff and the interests and abilities of the physical education department have low loadings but contribute to the naming of the factor as *community resources*.

Factor 4

The highest loading is on item 4 which refers to the provision of adequate facilities. Lower loadings relate to adequate financial provision, time-table allocation and the age of the children. The factor is named *school resources*.

Factor 5

The major loading, item 15, is concerned with the needs of society. Lower loadings on items 11, 13, 14 and 17 embrace cultural and social factors in the community. The factor is concerned with societal influences and is named *societal values*.

Factor 6

The highest loading on item 12, the democratic discussion with physical education staff, supported by the much lower loadings of the ability to offer choice in the programme at some stage and the aims of the subject, contributed to the naming of this factor as *democratic atmosphere*.

Factor 7

This factor is apparently concerned with the children. The high loading on the range of abilities within classes (item 19) and the lower loading related to the interests and needs of the children (item 20) contribute to the naming of this factor as *children's abilities and interests.*

Purposes of planning

The fourteen items from the questionnaire and their loadings on the four abstracted factors are set out in Table D.2. The interpretations and naming of the factors are inferred from the loadings.

Factor 1

This large factor accounts for 24% of the variance. Moderate loadings are recorded against five items (7, 8, 12, 13 and 14) and low loadings on two items (6 and 11). All the variables are related to the efficiency in the department and the subject organization. The factor is named *co-ordination and continuity.*

Factor 2

Only one item (9) has a high loading on this factor and is concerned with guidance for the children. A minor loading relates to teaching methods (item 3). The factor appears to be related to *guidance for children.*

Factor 3

Items 4 and 5 have high loadings which are concerned with the needs of children while at school and once they have left school. The factor is described as *children's needs.*

Factor 4

A high loading is recorded for item 1 and a moderate loading for item 2. These variables describe guidance for the subject as well as for the physical education staff. The factor is named *subject guide for staff.*

Methods of evaluation

The factor analysis computed on the fifteen items on the ways in which teachers judge the success of their curriculum planning is set out in Table D.3.

Table D.2. Purposes of Planning: Variables & Rotated Component Loadings.

Component loadings*

Item	Variable	1	2	3	4
1	As a guide to the PE staff	24	−06	01	63
2	As a guide to the subject	02	15	−08	51
3	As a way of suggesting teaching methods	11	31	15	27
4	As a consideration of children's needs whilst at school	27	10	62	−01
5	As a consideration of children's needs once they have left school	07	15	71	−01
6	To ensure efficient use of resources and facilities	34	06	07	06
7	To ensure continuity in teaching	42	04	17	28
8	To state the aims of PE	51	21	−08	13
9	As a guide to the children	17	83	07	01
10	To utilize staff expertise	18	28	13	06
11	To be consistent with school philosophy	36	29	10	06
12	To enable Head of Dept. to co-ordinate work	43	04	09	34
13	To provide suitable learning experiences	56	12	25	01
14	To ensure adequate evaluation	53	23	16	12
	Cumulative % variance	24.3	35.1	43.5	51.4

* Decimal point omitted; loadings rounded to two places.

Table D.3. Methods of Evaluation: Variables & Rotated Component Loadings.

Component loadings*

Item	Variable	1	2	3	4	5
1	Maintaining school traditions	−07	16	51	00	03
2	Participation in post school recreation	−02	59	15	03	06
3	Objective measurement	28	02	21	03	32
4	Subjective opinion	24	−06	10	20	24
5	Enjoyment	11	30	07	25	−11
6	Development of good attitudes	08	31	−02	54	10
7	Working atmosphere	10	03	06	68	12
8	Skill levels	−05	−02	−07	18	61
9	Success in external competition	03	11	45	−02	12
10	Fitness levels	11	23	15	−05	50
11	Extra-curricular participation	05	40	12	10	10
12	Social competence	50	33	−02	18	07
13	Aesthetic appreciation	80	−01	07	08	05
14	Parental interest	34	33	35	04	−01
15	Other teachers' opinions	20	02	50	12	−03
	Cumulative % variance	19.1	29.2	38.4	47.1	54.4

* Decimal point omitted; loadings rounded to two places.

The loadings on the five abstracted factors are used to interpret and name the factors.

Factor 1

A high loading is recorded against aesthetic appreciation (item 13), a moderate loading against social competence and a low loading against parental interest (items 12 and 14). The interpretation of this factor is concerned with *aesthetic and social appreciation.*

Factor 2

The loadings on this factor show an emphasis on participation in post school (item 2) and extra-curricular activity (item 11). Minor loadings on enjoyment, the development of good attitudes, parental interest and social competence (items 5, 6, 12 and 14) support the notion that this factor is concerned with *leisure participation.*

Factor 3

The main loadings on this factor are concerned with maintaining school traditions (item 1), success in external competition (item 9) and other teachers' opinions (item 15). A minor loading on item 14 relates to parental interest. Taken together, the interrelationship of these items appear to be concerned with the standards within the physical education department. The factor is therefore named *standards.*

Factor 4

Item 7 received the highest loading and is concerned with the working atmosphere. The development of good attitudes (item 6) is also substantially linked to this factor. The factor is named *climate.*

Factor 5

The highest loading is on item 8, skill levels, with a moderate loading on item 10, fitness levels, and a low loading on item 3, objective measurement. The interpretation of this factor is concerned with *motor development.*

Bibliography

ALMOND, L. (1975) 'Alternative approaches in curriculum planning', *B.J. Physical Ed.* 6. May/June. 44.

ALMOND, L. (1976) 'Teacher involvement in curriculum planning', in KANE, J.E. (Ed.) *Curriculum development in physical education.* Crosby Lockwood Staples.

AMERICAN ALLIANCE FOR HEALTH, P.E. AND RECREATION (1977) *Assessment Guide for Secondary School Physical Education Programs.* AAHPER.

AMIDON, E.J. and HOUGH, J.B. (Eds.) (1967) *Interaction Analysis: Theory, Research and Application.* Addison Wesley.

ANDERSON, W.G. (1971) 'Descriptive analytic research on teaching', *Quest.* Monograph XV. 1–8.

ANDERSON, W.G. (1980) *Analysis of Teaching Physical Education.* C.V. Mosby.

ANDERSON, W.G. and BARRETTE, G.T. (Eds.) (1978) 'What's going on in gym? Descriptive studies of physical education classes', Monograph 1 of *Motor Skills: Theory into Practice.* Newtown, Conn.

ANDREWS, B.H. (1976) 'The role of physical education in the whole curriculum', *Research Papers in P.E.* 3.2. 47–49.

ANDREWS, J. (1979) *Essays on Physical Education and Sport.* Stanley Thornes.

ARMSTRONG, G.N. (1976) Aspects of curriculum development. *B.J. Physical Ed.* 7. Sept/Oct. xLi.

BIGLIN, B. (1976) 'Enjoyment, the primary objective?' *B.J. Physical Ed.* 7. Nov/Dec. 110.

BLOOM, B.S. (Ed.) (1956) *The Taxonomy of Educational Objectives. 1. Cognitive Domain.* McKay.

BONDI, J.C. (1970) 'Feedback from interaction analysis: some implications for the improvement of teaching', *J. Teacher Educ.* 21. 2. 189–196.

BROWN, G. (1975) *Micro-teaching: A Programme of Teaching Skills.* Methuen.

CARROLL, R. (1976) 'Physical education teachers' own evaluation of their lessons', *Journal of Psycho-Social Aspects.* Occasional Papers No.2.

CARROLL, R. (1981) 'CSE in physical education – an evaluation', *Bulletin of Physical Education.* 17.1. 5–17.

CARROLL, T.E. (1974) 'A rational curriculum plan for physical education', *B.J. Physical Ed.* 5. Nov/Dec. 103.

CHEFFERS, J.T.F. (1972) The validation of an instrument design to expand the Flanders system of interaction analysis to describe non-verbal interaction, different varieties of teacher behaviour and pupil responses. Unpublished doctoral dissertation. Temple University.

CHEFFERS, J.T.F. (1977) Systematic observation in teaching. Paper presented at the AIESEP International Conference. Madrid.

CHEFFERS, J.T.F. and LOMBARDO, B.J. (1979) 'The observation and description of teaching behaviour and interaction of selected physical education teachers', *Resources in Education* (ERIC). Document ED 173325.

CLARK, C.M. and YINGER, R.J. (1979) 'Teachers thinking', in PETERSON, P.L. and WALBERG, H.J. (Eds.) *Research on Teaching: Concepts, Findings and Implications.* McCutchan.

CLEGG, A. (1975) 'Battery fed and factory tested', *Times Educational Supplement.* 11 July.

COPE, E. (1975) 'Evaluation in physical education', *Journal of Psycho-Social Aspects.* Occasional Papers No.1.

COSTELLO, J. and LAUBACH, S.A. (1978) 'Student behaviour', in ANDERSON, W.G. and BARRETTE, G.T. (Eds.) What's going on in gymn? Descriptive studies of physical education classes. Monograph 1 of *Motor Skills: Theory into Practice.* Newtown, Conn. 11–24.

CRATTY, B.J. (1973) *Movement Behaviour and Motor Learning.* Lea and Febiger.

DAVIES, I.K. (1976) *Objectives in Curriculum Design.* McGraw-Hill.

DELAMONT, S. and HAMILTON, D. (1976) 'Classroom research: a critique and a new approach', in STUBBS, M. and DELAMONT, S. (Eds.) *Explorations in Classroom Observations.* Wiley.

DEPARTMENT OF EDUCATION AND SCIENCE (1977) *Curriculum 11–16.* Working papers by H.M. Inspectorate: a contribution to current debate. HMSO.

DEPARTMENT OF EDUCATION AND SCIENCE (1980) *A View of the Curriculum.* HMI Series: Matters for Discussion 11. HMSO.

DEPARTMENT OF EDUCATION AND SCIENCE (1981) *The School Curriculum.* HMSO.

DOUGHERTY, N.J. (1971) 'A plan for the analysis of teacher-pupil interaction in physical education classes', *Quest.* Monograph XV. 39–50.

DROWATZKY, J.N. (1975) *Motor Learning: Principles and Practices.* Burgess.

DYBALL, M. (1976) 'Balance of physical education in the curriculum', *Research Papers in Physical Education.* 3.2. 50–51.

ECKERT, H.M. (1974) *Practical Measurement of Physical Performance.* Lea and Febiger.

EISNER, E.W. (1969) 'Instructional and expressive educational objectives: their formulations and use in curriculum', in POPHAM, W.J. *et al* (Eds.) *Instructional Objectives.* AERA Monograph 3. Rand McNally.

EISNER, E.W. (1979) 'Qualitative education to improve practice'. Lecture delivered at the Institute of Education, University of London.

ERAUT, M., GOAD, L. and SMITH, G. (1975) *The Analysis of Curriculum Materials.* University of Sussex Education Area. Occasional Paper No.2.

EVANS, K.M. (1968) *Planning Small-Scale Research.* NFER.

FISHMAN, S.E. and ANDERSON, W.G. (1971) 'Developing a system for describing teaching', *Quest.* Monograph XV. 9–16.

FLANDERS, N.A. (1967) 'The problems of observer training and reliability', in AMIDON, E.J. and HOUGH, J.B. (Eds.) *Interaction Analysis: Theory, Research and Application.* Addison Wesley.

FLANDERS, N.A. (1970) *Analyzing Teaching Behavior.* Addison Wesley.

FORD TEACHING PROJECT (1975) Centre for Applied Research in Education. University of East Anglia.

GALTUNG, J. (1967) *Theory and Methods of Social Research.* Allen and Unwin.

GENTILE, A.M. (1972) 'A working model of skill acquisition with application to teaching', *Quest.* 17. 3–23.

GIBSON, D.R. (1970) 'Classroom observation using video tapes', *Bulletin*, Un. of London. 20. 31–34.

GLAISTER, I.K. (Ed.) (1976) *Evaluation in Physical Education.* NATFHE. Physical Education Section. Conference Report.

GOLBY, M., GREENWALD, J. and WEST, R. (Eds.) (1975) *Curriculum Design.* Croom Helm.

GRAHAM, G.M. (1975) 'A bridge between "What Is" and "What Could be",' *Physical Educator*. 32.1. 14–17.

HEINILA, L. (1979) 'Analyzing systems in the evaluation of the teacher-pupil interaction process in physical education classes', in TAMMIVUORI, T. (Ed.) *Evaluation in the Development of Physical Education*. International Congress of Physical Education. Finnish Society for Research in Sport and Physical Education.

HENDRY, L.B. (1978) *School, Sport and Leisure*. Lepus.

HOGBEN, D. (1972) 'The behavioural objectives approach: some problems and dangers', *J. Curric. Studies*. 4. 42–50.

HOOPER, R. (Ed.) (1971) *The Curriculum: Context, Design and Development*. Oliver and Boyd.

HOPKINSON, J. (1976) 'Computers and sport', *Computer Ed.* 24. Nov. 30–31.

HOSTE, R. (1976) 'Evaluating the physical education course' in GLAISTER, I.K. (Ed.) *Evaluation in Physical Education*. NATFHE. Physical Education Section. Conference Report.

HURWITZ, R.F. (1973) 'The reliability and validity of descriptive-analytic systems for studying classroom behaviours', *Classroom Interaction Newsletter*. 8. 2. 50–59.

JAMES, B. (1978) 'Evaluation in a physical education department', *Bulletin of Physical Education*. XIV. 1. 23–33.

JEWETT, A.E. and NORTON, C. (Eds.) (1979) Curriculum theory conference in physical education. Conference Proceedings. University of Georgia.

JONES, L. (1975) 'Secondary music teachers' attitudes towards the teaching of their subject', *J. Curric. Studies*. 7.1. 55–68.

JORDAN, T.C. (1971) 'Micro-teaching: a reappraisal of its value in teacher education', *Quest*. Monograph XV. 17–21.

KANE, J.E. (1974) *Physical Education in Secondary Schools*. Macmillan.

KANE, J.E. (Ed.) (1976) *Curriculum Development in Physical Education*. Crosby Lockwood Staples.

KANE, J.E. (Ed.) (1977) *Movement Studies and Physical Education*. Routledge & Kegan Paul.

KEELE INTEGRATED STUDIES PROJECT (1973) Schools Council Integrated Studies. Oxford University Press.

KELLY, A.V. (1977) *The Curriculum: Theory and Practice*. Harper and Row.

KERLINGER, F.N. (1973) *Foundations of Behavioural Research*. Holt, Rinehart & Winston.

KIRK, P.M. (1976) 'The role of physical education in the whole curriculum', *Research Papers in Physical Education*. 3.2. 44–46.

KNAPP, B. (1963) *Skill in Sport: The Attainment of Proficiency*. Routledge and Kegan Paul.

KNIGHT, R.F. and SCOTT, S. (1970) 'Ohio-Michigan conference on curriculum improvement in secondary physical education', *J. Health Phys. Educ. Recreation*. 41. 1. 57–60.

KRATHWOHL, D.R., BLOOM, B.S. and MASIA, B.B. (1964) *Taxonomy of Educational Objectives. II Affective Domain*. Longman.

LAWTHER, J.D. (1968) *The Learning of Physical Skills*. Prentice Hall.

LAWTON, D. (1973) *Social Change, Educational Theory and Curriculum Planning*. University of London Press.

LAWTON, D., GORDON, P., ING. M., GIBBY, W.A., PRING, R. and MOORE, T. (1978) *Theory and Practice of Curriculum Studies*. Routledge and Kegan Paul.

LINES, V.M. (1976) 'Balance of physical education in the curriculum', *Research Papers in Physical Education*. 3. 2. 52–54.

LOGSDON, B.J. (Ed.) (1977) *Physical Education for Children: A Focus on the Teaching Process*. Lea and Febiger.

LUFF, I.V. (1980) 'Curriculum evaluation: a neglected process?', *Phys. Educ. Rev.* 3. 1. 18–33.

MARTENIUK, R.G. (1976) *Information Processing in Motor Skills.* Holt, Rinehart and Winston.

MACDONALD, B. and WALKER, R.R. (1975) 'Case-study and the social philosophy of educational research', *Cambridge J. of Educ.* 5.1 Lent Term. 2–11.

MCGLYNN, G.H. (1974) *Issues in Physical Education and Sports.* National Press Books.

MCINTOSH (1963) *Sport in Society.* C.A. Watts and Co. Ltd.

MCINTYRE, D.I. (1980) 'Systematic observation of classroom activities' in HARGREAVES, D.H. (Ed.) Classroom studies. *Educational Analysis.* 2.2. 3–30.

M.C.C. (1976) *The M.C.C. Cricket Coaching Book.* Heinemann.

MELOGRANO, V. (1979) *Designing Curriculum and Learning: A Physical Co-education Approach.* Kendall-Hunt.

MORGAN, R.E. (1974) *Concerns and Values in Physical Education.* G. Bell & Sons.

MOSER, C. and KALTON, G. (1979) *Survey Methods in Social Investigation.* Heinemann.

MOSSTON, M. (1966) *Teaching Physical Education.* Charles E. Merrill.

MOSSTON, M. (1972) *Teaching: From Command to Discovery.* Wadsworth.

MUNROW, A.D. (1972) *Physical Education – A Discussion of Principles.* G. Bell and Sons.

NICHOLLS, A. and H. (1972) *Developing a Curriculum: A Practical Guide.* Allen and Unwin.

NIE, N.H., HULL, C.H., JENKINS, J.G., STEINBRENNER, K. and BENT, D.H. (1975) *Statistical Package for the Social Sciences.* McGraw-Hill.

NIXON, J.E. and LOCKE, L.F. (1973) Research on teaching physical education in TRAVERS, R.M.W. (Ed.) *Second Handbook of Research on Teaching.* Rand McNally.

OKUNROTIFA, P.O. (1976) 'The effect of stating behavioural objectives on class performance and retention in geography', *J. Curric. St.* 8.1. 79–84.

OPPENHEIM, A.N. (1966) *Questionnaire Design and Measurement.* Heinemann.

ORLOSKY, D.R. and SMITH, B.O. (Eds.) (1978) *Curriculum Development: Issues and Insights.* Rand McNally.

OXENDINE, J.B. (1968) *Psychology of Motor Learning.* Appleton Century Crofts.

PALMER, R. (1978) 'Physical education in schools: current issues and solutions', *Physical Education Review.* 1. 101–110.

PARLETT, M. and HAMILTON, D. (1976) 'Evaluation as illumination' in TAWNEY, D. (Ed.) *Curriculum Evaluation To-day: Trends and Implications.* Schools Council. Macmillan.

PARSONS, C.J. (1973) *Theses and Project Work.* Allen & Unwin.

PATE, R. and CORBIN, C. (1981) 'Health related physical fitness test. Implications for the curriculum', *J. of Physical Ed. and Rec.* Jan. 36–38.

PIERON, M. (Ed.) (1978) *Towards a Science of Teaching Physical Education: Teaching Analysis.* AIESEP

PIERON, M. and HACOURT, J. (1979) 'Teaching behaviours at different levels of physical education teaching', *Bulletin of the International Federation of Physical Education.* 49. 2. 3–11.

PIERON, M. and HANN, J.M. (1980) 'Pupils activities, time on task and behaviours in high school physical education teaching', *Bulletin of the International Federation of Physical Education.* 50. 3/4. 62–68.

POLIDORO, J.R. (1976) 'Performance objectives: a practical approach toward accountability', *Physical Educator.* 33.1. 20–23.

POULTON, E.C. (1957) 'On prediction in skilled movements', *Psychol. Bull.* 54. 6. 467–478.

PRING, R. (1973) 'Objectives and innovation: the irrelevance of theory', *London Educational Review.* 2. 3. 46–54.

RICHMOND, W.K. (1971) *The School Curriculum.* Methuen.

ROSENSHINE, B. and FURST, N. (1973) 'The use of direct observation to study teaching' in TRAVERS, R.M.W. (Ed.) *Second Handbook of Research on Teaching*. Rand McNally.

ROSS, J.M. (1973) 'The physical education departments of 12 comprehensive schools', *B.J. Physical Ed.* 4. March/April. ix–xii.

RUGBY FOOTBALL UNION (1966) *A Guide for Coaches*. RFU.

SAGE, G.H. (1971) *An Introduction to Motor Behaviour: A Neuropsychological Approach*. Addison Wesley.

SCHILLING, G. and BAUR, W. (Eds.) (1980) *Audiovisual Means in Sport*. Birkhäuser Verlag.

SCHOOLS COUNCIL (1968–72) *Middle Years of Schooling*. Working paper No.22. HMSO.

SCHOOLS COUNCIL (1970–81) *Engineering Science*.

SCHOOLS COUNCIL (1970–81) *Geography for the Young School Leaver*.

SCHOOLS COUNCIL (1978–1986) *Evaluation and the Teacher*.

SCOTT, W.A. (1955) 'Reliability of content analysis: the case of nominal scale coding', *Public Opinion Quarterly*. 19. 321–325.

SEIDEL, B.L. and RESICK, M.C. (1978) *Physical Education: An Overview*. Addison Wesley.

SILVESTER, P.J. (1971) 'Curriculum development and physical education'. *B.J. Physical Ed.* 2. March/April. 17–19.

SINGER, R.N. (1975) *Motor Learning and Human Performance*. Macmillan.

SINGER, R.N. (Ed.) (1976) *Physical Education: Foundations*. Holt, Rinehart and Winston.

SINGER, R.N. and DICK, W. (1974) *Teaching Physical Education: A Systems Approach*. Houghton Mifflin.

SMITH, D.L. and FRASER, B.J. (1980) 'Towards a confluence of quantitative and qualitative approaches to curriculum evaluation', *J. Curric. St.* 12.4. 367–370.

SOCKETT, H. (1976) *Designing the Curriculum*. Open Books.

STENHOUSE, L. (1970) 'Some limitations of the use of objectives in curriculum research and planning', *Pedagogica Europea*. 6. 73–83.

STENHOUSE, L. (1975) *An Introduction to Curriculum Research and Development*. Heinemann.

TABA, H. (1962) *Curriculum Development: Theory and Practice*. Harcourt Brace.

TAMMIVUORI, T. (Ed.) (1979) *Evaluation in the Development of Physical Education*. The Finnish Society for Research in Sport and Physical Education. Publication 64.

TAVECCHIO, L.W.C. (1977) *Quantification of Teaching Behaviour in Physical Education*. VRB drukkerijen.

TAWNEY, D. (1976) *Curriculum Evaluation To-day: Trends and Implications*. Schools Council. Macmillan.

TAYLOR, P.H. (1970) *How Teachers Plan Their Courses*. NFER.

TAYLOR, P.H. (1976) 'Explorations in the concept of evaluation' in GLAISTER, I.K. (Ed.) *Evaluation in Physical Education*. NATFHE. Physical Education Section. Conference Report.

TEMPLIN, P.J. (1978) 'Understanding life within physical education: an ethnographic approach', *Resources in Education*. (ERIC) Document ED 148796.

TRAVERS, R.M.W. (Ed.) (1973) *Second Handbook of Research on Teaching*. Rand McNally.

TYLER, R.W. (1949) *Basic Principles of Curriculum and Instruction*. University of Chicago Press.

UNDERWOOD, G.L. (1974) 'Leadership in physical education', *Bulletin of Physical Education*. X. 2. 11–17.

UNDERWOOD, G.L. (1977) 'Curriculum planning and development', in KANE, J.E. (Ed.) *Movement Studies and Physical Education*. Routledge and Kegan Paul.

UNDERWOOD, G.L. (1978) The rationale of curriculum planning. Paper presented at P.E.A. Conference, London.

UNDERWOOD, G.L. (1978) 'An investigation into the teaching of a basketball lesson using interaction analysis techniques', in PIERON, M. (Ed.) *Towards a Science of Teaching Physical Education*. AIESEP. 77–88.

UNDERWOOD, G.L. (1980) 'A comparison of direct and problem-solving approaches in the teaching of physical education', in SCHILLING, G. and BAUR, W. (Eds.) *Audiovisual Means in Sport*. Birkhäuser Verlag, 285–295.

VOGEL, P. (1969) 'Battle Creek physical education project', *J. Health Phys. Educ. Recreation*. 40. 7. 25–29.

WALKER, R. and ADELMAN, C. (1975) 'Interaction analysis in informal classrooms: a critical comment on the Flanders' system', *B.J. Ednl. Psych*. 45. 73–76.

WALKER, R. and ADELMAN, C. (1976) 'Strawberries' in STUBBS, M. and DELAMONT, S. (Eds.) *Explorations in Classroom Observation*. Wiley.

WELSH, R. (Ed.) (1977) *Physical Education: A View Toward the Future*. C.V. Mosby.

WHEELER, D.K. (1967) *Curriculum Process*. University of London Press.

WHITEHEAD, N.J. and HENDRY, L.B. (1976) *Teaching Physical Education in England – Description and Analysis*. Lepus Books.

WHITING, H.T.A. (1969) *Acquiring Ball Skill: A Psychological Interpretation*. Lea and Febiger.

WILHELMS, F.T. (1971) 'Evaluation as feedback', in HOOPER, R. (Ed.) *The Curriculum: Context, Design and Development*. Oliver and Boyd.

WRAGG, E.C. (1970) 'Interaction analysis as a feedback system for student teachers', *Education for Teaching*. 81. 38–47.

ZAHORIK, J.A. (1970) 'The effect of planning on teaching', *Elementary School Journal*. 71. 143–151.

ZAHORIK, J.A. (1975) 'Teachers' planning models', *Educational Leadership*. 33. 134–139.

Author Index

Subject Index